Children of Atlantis

Voices from the Former Yugoslavia

Translations and standardization

of the English text

by

Christina Pribićević-Zorić

_____

Children of Atlantis

Voices from the Former Yugoslavia

Edited by Zdenko Lešić

Central European University Press

Budapest ♦ London ♦ New York

British Library Cataloguing in Publication Data
A CIP catalogue record for this book is available from the British Library

ISBN 1-85866-041-6 Paperback

Library of Congress Cataloguing in Publication Data
A CIP catalog record for this book is available from the Library of Congress

Published by
Central European University Press
H-1051 Budapest, Nádor u. 9, Hungary

Distributed by
Oxford University Press, Walton Street, Oxford OX2 6DP
Oxford New York Athens Auckland Bangkok Bombay Toronto Calcutta Cape Town
Dar es Salaam Delhi Florence Hong Kong Istanbul Karachi Kuala Lumpur Madras
Madrid Melbourne Mexico City Nairobi Paris Singapore Taipei Tokyo Toronto
and associated companies in Berlin Ibadan
Distributed in the United States by Oxford University Press Inc., New York

Produced by Ari Korpivaara
Designed by Jeanne Criscola
Printed in the United States by W.E. Andrews of Connecticut, Inc.

Text set in ITC Esprit by Jovica Veljović
Printed on recycled paper

Cover photo: ©Gilles Peress, *Farewell to Bosnia*, 1994

Contents

Part I
Stories of War and Exile

Part II
Stories of Disillusionment, Despair and Hope

Preface

In the spring and summer of 1992, in various parts of the world, young people uprooted by the war in the former Yugoslavia began to make enquiries about the possibility of continuing their education in the countries where they had sought refuge. Some resourceful individuals were able to find solutions and engage in negotiations with universities on their own. Others turned to institutions for advice. In Austria, Dr Wolfgang Benedek at the World University Service, Graz, began to realize the scale of the problem and undertake action on behalf of the many refugee students in his country. Through him, the World University Service, Austria, organized jointly with ESIB (the National Union of Students in Europe) and the Croatian Students' Parliament a meeting in Zagreb in June 1993. In the UK Celia Hawkesworth launched a campaign, based at the School of Slavonic and East European Studies, University of London, to encourage institutions of higher education to make available one free place for refugee students from the former Yugoslavia and to raise funds for their maintenance. She worked closely with the European Educational and Cultural Institute of Bosnia and Herzegovina, a London-based organization founded to help refugees continue their education.

At the same time, foundations established and funded by George Soros around the world, and particularly the Open Society Fund in New York, were receiving growing numbers of enquiries about possible financial support for refugee students. In the autumn of 1992, Beka Vučo, a New York–based foundation executive director with responsibility for the foundations in the former Yugoslavia, secured a grant from the Open Society Fund to assist the UK operation and began to formulate ideas for a worldwide programme. Pursuing other avenues, in November 1993 Dr Benedek organized a meeting in Graz to discuss the problem with several interested parties, including the Council of Europe. The Council took up the issue and itself organized a meeting in Strasbourg in February 1994. One of the resolutions adopted on this occasion was that the matter should be brought before European Ministers of Education. This action was supported by the Secretary General, Mme Catherine Lalumière, and led to the question being considered in Strasbourg in April 1994 at the Council of Europe's Committee on Higher Education and Research. Among other proposals, the Committee was asked to assist refugee students. As a result of this meeting, the Conference of Rectors of European Universities also agreed to set up a Task Force to consider ways of supporting universities in the former Yugoslavia.

By February 1994, the Open Society Institute Supplementary Grant Program for Students from the Former Yugoslavia had been launched in a number of countries where it was known that there were significant groups of refugee students. Beka Vučo assembled an international board, consisting of representatives from France (Dr Rada Iveković, formerly of the University of Zagreb, currently in Paris), Holland (Dragan Klaić, formerly from the Theatre Academy in Belgrade, currently in Amsterdam), the UK (Celia Hawkesworth, University of London) and the USA (Dr Karen J. Greenberg, Vice President for Programs, Open Society Institute; Dr Vesna Najfeld, originally from Belgrade, now working in New York). Dr Wolfgang Benedek, of WUS, Austria, was later invited to join the Board. The Board met in New York in February to consider the first batch of applications, for the remainder of the school year 1993–94. It was clear then that regional sub-committees would have to be established to deal with the expected volume of applications for the school year 1994–95. These were set up and the applications began to flood in. By the closing date, in April 1994, nearly 2,000 had been received. The sub-committees worked very hard to process them in time for the Board meeting in July. A total of 1,134 grants were awarded for 1994–95, distributed as follows: Austria: 262; UK: 198; Albania: 153; USA: 144; France: 109; Germany: 85; Czech Republic: 55; Israel: 37; Holland: 22; Spain: 17; Romania: 14; Canada: 13; Italy: 7; Switzerland: 7; Slovakia: 5; Norway: 2; Portugal: 2; Belarus: 1; Cyprus: 1.

As this volume goes to press, applications are beginning to come in for the 1995–96 school year. The Open Society Institute has again made a generous provision to the scholarship grant programme and we are hoping to be able to meet at least the most urgent needs for assistance.

While the primary aim of the Grant Program is to enable hundreds of talented young people, whose lives have been disrupted through no fault of their own, to continue their education, it has another dimension, regarded by the Board as equally important. From the outset, it was clear that these young people represented an irreplaceable human resource which had to be fostered, firstly in order to salvage whatever possible from their positive earlier experience of peaceful, happy, multicultural living, growing up in Yugoslavia. This was something that the students all took for granted: for the most part it had not occurred to them to wonder about the ethnic background of their friends and colleagues. We feel that the intrinsically positive value of this experience must be cherished as they will carry it with them throughout their lives, wherever they may be, and it is our task to ensure that it is not corroded by the bitterness and anger that are inevitably engendered by war. Secondly, it is our shared hope that sooner or later, whenever conditions permit, many of these talented youngsters will return to make an important contribution towards recreating the intellectual life of their countries. The knowledge and skills they have acquired during their enforced exile will be invaluable in the societies that ultimately emerge from the war, and their experience of living in different social systems can offer a vital source of strength and confidence in the process of building open, tolerant, democratic societies.

Reading the applications of candidates for Supplementary Grants, the Board members were impressed by the depth of their commitment to fundamental human values, eloquently expressed in the extracts printed here. This testimony to a generation cast out of their homeland bears witness to the wanton destruction of a uniquely precious resource and hence to another, less visible, aspect of the sickening waste of war. It will take many future generations to recreate what is represented here.

Celia Hawkesworth

Introduction

It was Plato who introduced the image of Atlantis to the collective human imagination. Atlantis, he said, was a rich land of happy people which disappeared into the waters of the ocean, possibly in the wake of some devastating earthquake. He never asked himself whether anyone had survived the country's collapse. According to a later legend, some of Atlantis's inhabitants did manage to save themselves, and like castaways were washed ashore on the Atlantic coast of southern Europe. But this legend says nothing about how these unhappy children of Atlantis felt when disgorged by the ocean onto unfamiliar, foreign shores. (Legends never dwell on feelings, because feelings belong to the intimate world of the individual, whereas legends are about the experience of the collective.) But if one thinks of the Iberian Basques as possible descendants of that legendary lost land, then it is not hard to imagine how lost the survivors of Atlantis must have felt, for in the world they encountered they were to remain forever foreign and misunderstood. Perhaps those children of Atlantis felt like the many Yugoslavs ('ex-Yugoslavs', 'former Yugoslavs', 'post-Yugoslavs') who found themselves in a foreign world after their country's violent disintegration. Cast onto foreign shores by the convulsive waves of war, left without a home or homeland, they are condemned to live an archetypal experience, the experience of people who have suddenly lost their country.

Children of Atlantis, composed of 'voices from the former Yugoslavia', brings this experience to light. In so doing, in revealing the psychological aspects of such a modern historical disaster as the war in the former Yugoslavia, this book also highlights an age-old human experience of almost mythic proportions: the feelings of people bereft of their home and homeland.

The brutal war in the Balkans has forced more than two million people into exile. Many of them are young; they interrupted their education, left their parents and homes to get away from the vicissitudes of war and the life it imposes. Arriving in a foreign country, they were initially just glad to be alive. But then, almost invariably, they began to feel lost, helpless, disillusioned and deceived. Within only a short period of time, the pressure of nationalism and the aggression of war had changed the face of their homeland and, like some monster, it had begun to devour its own children. Stunned by the explosion of nationalist frenzy, frightened by the force of the hatred and anger, appalled by the horrors of war, faced with the risk of being mobilized and fearing for their very lives, they left their country in search of shelter elsewhere. Shelter they found, but it meant becoming refugees. They ceased being what they were used to being. Along with the loss of personal happiness, they lost their personal identities as well. They foundered in the collective misery of people without a homeland or home. They joined the army of 'exiles', 'the displaced', 'refugees' and 'asylum-seekers' spewed out in waves from all corners of the world by modern human history, their fate unresolved by today's world.

Still, many of them have found their way in these foreign lands. With the vitality so characteristic of the young (especially from their part of the world), they have survived and got on with their lives. Some have even continued their education. They have been greatly helped in this regard by the Open Society Institute and its programme of grants for students from the former Yugoslavia. This book assembles extracts from some of the essays written by students from the former Yugoslavia who applied for an Open Society Institute stipend, essays in which they explain the circumstances which prompted them to leave their country.

The students were asked to reply to the following questions in their essays:

1) 'What are your reasons for leaving the former Yugoslavia and your reasons for wanting to continue your education abroad?'

2) 'How do you perceive your future and the possibility of returning to your home country after your studies are completed?'

These two questions seem to have struck a painful chord with these young people who had been forced to leave their country and scatter all over the world. Provoked, they opened their hearts. In the essays they enclosed with their applications they used plain language. They did not philosophize. (They did not want to be deep.) They did not politicize. (They did not want to be politically 'mature' or 'correct'.) They did not analyse. (They did not want to explain what had happened.) Instead, they opened their hearts, presented their 'case', told their story. Not in the form of a literary essay, smooth in style, brilliant in thought, rich in associations, witty and seductive. The majority paid scant attention to form or style, and their language is therefore dry and straightforward, even when writing in their mother tongue (although the majority wrote their essays in English). It is as if they were sure their 'case' spoke for itself and therefore needed no literary elaboration. For them 'to write' meant 'to reveal themselves', nothing more. And so their essays are not loquacious, they do not play on words, but they are eloquent and expressive all the same. Their simple, plain, direct words were not intended to impress or captivate, to be appealingly colourful, melodious or full of stylistic turns. They were merely meant to draw attention to their own particular 'case', to reveal the individual within the collective fate, and to make that story seen and known. When reading these essays, it takes just a little imagination and a bit of empathy to guess the complicated personal situations and states of mind that lie behind their words.

'All happy families are alike, but every unhappy family is unhappy in its own way,' says Tolstoy at the beginning of *Anna Karenina*. In the case of war-afflicted Yugoslav families that statement can be turned around, because for them happiness has become singularly rare whereas unhappiness is the same for everybody because it is the common rule. That makes all unhappy stories alike as well. ('All our stories will be alike,' one of the students predicts correctly.) Moreover, in all their stories (and the editor has read more than 1,500) one finds the same spiritual core, the same narrative 'kernel' wrapped inside these layers of individual experience. The paradigm of their stories can be found in a statement made by the young Zlata Filipović to the Paris correspondent of the paper *Borba*: 'My wish to leave Sarajevo, to get away from the war, came true. I managed to leave the hell of Sarajevo where you could be killed at any moment. I'm glad I'm alive, but the world I now live in is not my world and I keep feeling sad about what I had to leave behind. One day I hope to return.'[1] They left different parts of the former Yugoslavia but they all share the same basic, ambivalent feeling, a feeling of (short-lived) happiness to have survived the hell and (long-lasting) grief for everything they had to leave behind: a more or less happy childhood, their beloved home town, friends, parents, country, culture, customs, language.

Although their essays essentially tell the same story and express the same basic psychological states of mind, they still differ greatly. In the end, Tolstoy was right: all unhappy people are unhappy in their own way. (Indeed, therein lies the human dimension of tragedy: how-

1   *Borba* (Belgrade, 30–31 July 1994, p. 9).

ever universal the plot, every tragic tale is a story in itself.) The main difference between them, of course, lies in their own individual experience of the war in their country. Some found it hard to take the unpleasant, stifling political atmosphere—as in the case of most of the young people who left Serbia; others could not bear waiting in the shelters of their besieged towns, perhaps to die—as in the case of those who lived in Bosnia and the south-eastern parts of Croatia. Some were abroad when the war broke out and could no longer return home; others fled from home because of the horrors of war. Some left home of their own volition; others were driven away. Some were wounded in the war; others lost their closest relatives. Some left home in the hope of returning one day; others do not believe there will ever be room for them again in the ethnically cleansed regions of the newly emerging states. But whatever the circumstances of their departure from the former Yugoslavia, most of them now feel like the unhappy 'children of Atlantis', like people without a home or home country.

And so, although their stories may have the same narrative core and may express the same spirit, they are not monotonous. Even when they echo the same words, the same ideas, the same facts, they reflect different individual experiences within, and different personal attitudes towards, one and the same enormous human tragedy. The voices we hear in this book (and we hear almost one hundred) do indeed tell the same story and bear witness to the same misfortune. But they complement and tie in with each other, as if one was picking up where the other had left off, as if one was saying what the other had forgotten to say, as if one wanted to underscore what the other had merely touched upon. This polyphony of voices slowly reveals the full complexity of the situation to which these young people bear witness. It completes the picture of an entire generation which, at the very threshold of adulthood, lost all hope of a future and was brought face to face with the utter uncertainty of life.

As we listen to these voices, it should not matter whom they belong to, what part of the former Yugoslavia they come from, what nationality they are or what political convictions they hold. One of the reasons why the authors of these essays are identified only by their initials is to deter readers from reading their nationality into the texts and from trying to 'decipher' them ideologically. This is to avoid drawing conclusions like: 'Well, it's natural for a Serb to think like that' or 'That's just what a Muslim (Croat, Albanian, Romanian, Hungarian) would say'. These young people are not advocates of any national ideology. On the contrary, most of them are its victims. Or at least its fervent opponents. Readers must remember that it is the human soul speaking here, not some representative of a social, ethnic or religious group. And that is what we hope you will hear in these essays—not some ideological discourse but the human voice and the tormented human soul.

Of course, since these are *human* voices, one cannot entirely avoid ideological interpretations of these essays. Those who wish to do so will easily recognize two or three clear ideological positions.

First, many of these young people can be said to express what the new national states in the former Yugoslavia have derisively dubbed 'Yugo-nostalgia': 'I've always felt Yugoslav,' says one of them. 'Yugoslavia is always in my heart,' says another. But such statements should be read with caution. (Nationalists, of course, do not know how to read with caution. As in all else, they are rash, even in the conclusions they draw.) Because the 'Yugoslavia' they are talking about does not belong to any political or ideological discourse, but rather denotes an experience of existence itself. For them it means a way of life they knew and loved, a way of life that made them happy. For them, 'Yugoslavia' is not a political notion, charged with ideological connotations, it is the natural space occupied by their erstwhile lives, a space in which they were free to move and in which they enjoyed moving. They lived *there and then*, and they did not think, nor do they think today, about whether that space was an 'artificial creation', a 'historical piece of fiction' or an 'unnaturally born state'. They did not think about whether that state represented a 'definitive solution to the Serbian question' or an 'expanded Serbia' which, as such, was a 'prison of the nations'. These young people simply equate the former Yugoslavia with their former lives. From their present perspective as refugees, that life inevitably looks better and happier to them (perhaps more so than it actually was). And if they are nostalgic, then it is for the life they lived, not for the state they lived in. And if you tell them that they are wrong, that they lived a sham, that their 'Yugoslavia' was just a big lie, a political illusion, it will only increase, not lessen, their misery. Because, having lost all hope of a future, they will then have lost their past as well. And their memory of the past is often the only thing they have left and that is worth keeping.

Perhaps these young people are 'Yugo-nostalgics' because, as they say themselves, they come from 'mixed marriages'. In Yugoslavia 'ethnically mixed marriages' formed a category which had ideological connotations. (Its ideological meaning was taken to the extreme by a political party which at the last moment tried to 'save' Yugoslavia. It was called the Party of Mixed Marriages.) For many people, however, this became a fateful designation. Their parents being of different nationalities, these children suddenly became somehow 'impure'— neither pure Serbs, nor pure Croats (or Muslims). Once indifferent to their 'supranational nationality', suddenly they became tragic figures for whom there was now no room either 'here' or 'there'. Being neither 'ours' nor 'theirs', they became the 'bastards of Yugoslavia', as one national leader called them. Unlike others who found or will eventually find their place, and happiness, in one of the new national states, these young people have indeed become the 'children of Atlantis', people without a home or homeland. Of course, this could be seen as a marginal phenomenon (and indeed it is often deliberately marginalized) were it not for the fact that we are talking about several million people who have thus lost their place in the world.

But even when they are not the offspring of mixed marriages, these young people often long for the communal life that was deliberately destroyed in the war (and long before it). They long for the communal life of people of different origins and nationalities. And this brings us to the third guiding idea to be found in the majority of essays in this book. The most consistent here are the young people from Sarajevo. Because for them life together was a simple fact of everyday existence, and even today they think of it as the most appealing thing about their native city.

Indeed, more than any other city in the former Yugoslavia, it is Sarajevo which is present in this book. (And this is not just because the editor came from that city, and spent nearly two years sharing the tragedy of war with its people.) But here Sarajevo assumes a different presence than the one given to it by the international media for the past 1,000 days and more. Here it is present not as a place of horror and despair, death and devastation; not as a terrifying symbol of war in the former Yugoslavia; not as a 'metaphor of evil'. Sarajevo appears in these stories as an almost idyllic place of erstwhile, and still possible, human happiness. And no wonder, because it appears in the memories of people who, in exile, remember their carefree childhoods and all the joyful excitement of youth. They remember the city in which they grew up, fell in love, made friends, everyone living together, all of them, Serbs, Croats, Muslims, Jews, Montenegrins, and those from 'mixed marriages' (especially the latter). These memories, even if not always quite 'objective' and 'reliable', are especially valuable to us, because on various sides and for various reasons it is now being said that even Sarajevo was a big lie, that it has always been a place of hate and ethnic conflict and that it is now witnessing the historical issue of what has been in the making there for a long time. Now, when cause and effect are so easily confused, these young people's memories of 'prewar' Sarajevo remind us of what the world has started to forget—that what is being destroyed in Sarajevo is not just a city but an idea. What is deliberately being destroyed in Sarajevo—from without but also from within (less so in the latter case perhaps, but just as persistently)—is the complex fabric of a multinational, multireligious, multicultural community, a community which could be the 'preliminary draft for a future Europe' (as the French anthropologist Edgar Morin correctly observed). Sarajevo was a city which proved that life together is possible. If this were not true, as some today claim, then why work on killing it so viciously? What purpose would there be to its persistent destruction? 'Sarajevo was an amulet-city, entrusted to our keeping,' says the poet Vesna Krmpotić. 'We did not know how to defend that Sarajevo in all other Muslim, Croatian and Serbian homes, villages and towns. And that is why we lost the right to the Sarajevo of our communal life. Sarajevo is an awareness that is leaving us, because we did not protect it from the bulldog of our psyches, from the thugs we have trained since who knows when on the polygons of our underworld.'

Perhaps *that* Sarajevo still exists *there*, at the foot of its mountains, on the banks of its river. It certainly lives as such in the memories and hearts of these young people scattered the world over. To quote a Polish poet:

> and if the City falls but a single man escapes
> he will carry the City within himself
> he will be the City on the roads of exile...[2]

---

2   Zbigniew Herbert, *Report from the Besieged City and Other Poems* (translated by John and Bogdana Carpenter, Oxford University Press, 1987).

Only thus can one understand the paradox of the book's subtitle: *Voices from the Former Yugoslavia*. As we read the stories in this book, we do indeed hear voices from a land that is no more. Students wrote in from all over the world, from Great Britain, France, Germany, Austria, Spain, Portugal, the Czech Republic, Romania, the USA, Israel, from countries where they happened to be albeit not of their own volition or choice. But their voices resound from *within*, from the very heart of a land that is no more. And that makes them all the more valuable, for they testify to the space they echo, to the war in that space, to the traumas of that war, and especially to its psychological aspects.

But, in keeping with the intentions of the publisher, this book has a very important aim of its own. And that is to bear witness to an entire generation of young people who, because of the war in Yugoslavia, have lost their place in the world. It is an appeal to help these young people regain their place in their world. They deserve it.

Zdenko Lešić

In my opinion, one of the most tragic outcomes of events in the ex-Yugoslav region is that so many young, educated, 'normal' people, with open minds on life and the world, have left. Not for good, I hope.

D. L.
Rankweil, Austria

'Where are you from?'
'Yugoslavia.'
'Is there any such country?'
'No, but it's still where I come from.'

Part I

Stories of War and Exile

'I saw war, and I saw everything.'

Chapter 1: **Recollections**

All Our Stories Will Be Alike

I know. All our stories will be alike. We're lost, all of us. Soon we'll all disappear in the cloud of hatred that's raining down on us. They're trying to poison us with that hatred, to widen the gap between us, to separate us once and for all, for the sake of the big plans they have for us. But we young people didn't know we belonged to different nations, that now we have to separate according to 'nationality'. We've had to grow up, too soon, in just two years, and we're being forced not only to separate but to leave our home, where we all lived together. Why did we separate? Why did we leave our home?

When we left, not one of us thought it would be for so long. I certainly didn't. I saw war, and I saw everything. I had wanted to see something so different. Just the way my parents—where are they now?—had wanted me, their only child, their 'clever little girl', to see something beautiful and good. When the war started, for a long time we hoped that one of the big powers would come and calm our small bickering nations (i.e. national parties). But that didn't happen. I stayed too long on the Dalmatian coast, waiting for that big moment. Having fled my home town, I found I was a foreigner on a coast I had once called 'ours', where I had spent the best days of my childhood. I spent half a year there, half a year of hope, expectation; facing hatred and deep depression. It was hard for a twenty-one-year-old girl to decide whether everything she had believed in was a big lie, or whether the lie was in all the things they had started telling us a year or two before the war.

I had my religion. It was neither Islam nor Christianity. It was love. (I don't know who will read this and if they have ever been to Sarajevo. If not, they may not be able to understand.) What made life so special in our town was love, love among the people, and the love of Sarajevans for their city. Today it all seems like a dream. But I still feel that same love. And that is my religion. I am the richer and the stronger for it, because it is inside me. It is the source of my energy, of my will to live, and of my success at school. It gives me the strength to fight this battle called life.

I don't think I'm young any more. I'm twenty-three. But until very recently I was protected by maternal love and the security only a parent can give a beloved child. I wasn't prepared for 'life', certainly not for *this* kind of life, so far away from home. In the world I live in now, everything is different: the style of life, system of values, rhythm. I had to cope with everything all at once, without falling apart. Most of us have found our feet in this upheaval. I have. We've survived. But are we living or are we just surviving? We've developed the technique of everyday life in the UK: you follow the tracks laid out for you, although you're not on a train; you follow the road you know, but you don't know where it leads. I wonder whether any Sarajevan can be happy here. True, there is so much here that attracts the eye, you can't but enjoy it. But at night, when the curtains are pulled shut and it's bedtime, you begin to think and feel how inadequate your life is.

All of us studying here want to graduate. That's why we're here, at universities far away from home. But it's scary to think about what comes after that. Why? We wouldn't be happy staying here, following these same tracks. These past years we've been dreaming about going home. About restoring love to a city which is today shrouded in a cloud of hatred. To return love when it's most needed—that is my goal. Someone may ask: Why did you leave, then? But I didn't want to leave, they made me. And now I wonder: Will they let me go back?

Home, they say, is where you're happy. I was happy in Sarajevo.

S. R.
London, UK

Should I Stay or Should I Go?

Vlado walked into the classroom, raised two fingers high in the air and said: 'HDZ!'

Djordje was quick to answer, but instead of two, he raised three fingers and cried: 'SDS!'

Vedad did not even raise a finger. He just said: 'SDA!'

The tone of the conversation was humorous. I thought I must have missed part of the joke, so I just went along and laughed.

Later that evening, after I got home, I told my mum about it, hoping she would find it funny, laugh, and clarify the joke for me. I didn't want to tell her, or anyone else, that I didn't have a clue about what was going on. My mum did not laugh. She looked down and told me that she did not want to talk to me about such things. Mum had never said anything like that before. For the first time in my life I felt lost and confused.

Of course, it was just the beginning of everything that was to come. A few days later, students were asking each other about their nationalities. I remember hearing the words 'Serbs', 'Muslims', 'Croats', for the first time 'in the flesh'. I had heard them only in my classroom during lectures, or on television and radio. This time my friends were saying them.

Asked what my nationality was, I said: 'Yugoslav.'

'No, I mean really?' I heard a voice behind me say.

'Yugoslav,' I said again.

'Yes, but are you a Serb, a Muslim, a Croat, or what?' another voice broke in.

'I don't know,' I replied, confused.

They were laughing at me. I was really confused.

I was sixteen then, and felt that I had to find out more about this matter which seemed so important to everybody. This time I went to talk to my dad. Instead of an answer, I got a serious question: 'What do you think your nationality is?' 'Yugoslav,' I said, bowing my head as if I had said something shameful. 'Then, that is what you are!' my dad smiled.

My classmates were laughing at me, my dad was smiling. The whole thing puzzled me. This time I was not going to make a mistake. If anyone ever talked to me about anything seriously then it was Domagoj. I was not wrong. He told me that SDA, SDS and HDZ were political parties that represented, or supposedly represented, Muslims, Serbs and Croats respectively. That was good enough for a start.

A year passed by. The elections were over. In the meantime I had learned a lot about political parties, and politics. At least I thought I had. War was raging in Croatia. It was only a matter of time before Bosnia would start burning. But I did not know that then. Still, I felt that people had changed. Best friends were no longer best friends if they came from different ethnic or religious backgrounds.

My friend and I talked about the silliness of politics. We were afraid of being drafted into the army. We were only seventeen. But we discussed the matter seriously like adults. Some of us already had a way out, others knew they would not be able to avoid the draft, but nobody wanted to take a gun and shoot at a friend.

Two months passed. My dilemma was: 'Should I stay or should I go?' Many people had already left for Croatia, Serbia, or somewhere far away, where they could start their lives all over again. Then it happened.

It was a Tuesday. The basketball team for which I was playing had a game scheduled. During the day, the 'brains' of the team, including me, gathered to work out our strategy. And then I noticed that Domagoj was not there. Domagoj loved basketball. I felt as if I had been struck by lightning. I tried to get him on the phone. His dad answered. I went straight to the point and asked if I could speak to Domagoj. Silence at the other end of the line.

'He's not here,' a deep, sad voice finally replied.

I felt uneasy and asked one more question:

'Where is he?'

'He's far away,' the voice said. And I realized I might never see one of my best friends again.

'Domagoj did say something before he left,' continued the voice. 'He apologized for missing the game.'

I knew that it was a message for me.

I knew that Domagoj had not felt safe. I did not want to stay where my best friends could not feel safe. I had to go to some other place, where everyone can walk freely, where no one makes fun of or intimidates others simply because of their beliefs, nationality, or race.

I decided to find a school which I could attend without being interrogated by an armed guard, who suspects that my umbrella is a gun. In short, I decided to continue my education abroad. That is why I left Yugoslavia, Bosnia, or whatever that part of the world will be called by the time you read this.

But that is not the end of my story.

It was May 1993. I was in Emmett, Idaho, a small town in the middle of nowhere. I was getting ready to go to school when the phone rang. I picked it up and heard my dad's voice. Among other things he told me that Ferhadija had been destroyed. It caused me pain, but I was unable to cry. I remained motionless, like a stone. I don't remember the rest of the conversation. My dad's words kept echoing in my head: 'Ferhadija has gone…'

Originally Ferhadija was a mosque in Banja Luka. I say 'originally' because from the time it was built until the day it was destroyed its function had greatly changed. It was more than a religious institution. It was a symbol. Ferhadija saw a lot during its long lifetime, after the Muslims built it in the sixteenth century. In the early days it served the Turks for their religious ceremonies. But then the Turks left, and the Austrians came to rule over Bosnia. It was not an easy life for the old mosque. But the worst was yet to come. During the Second World War, when the Germans and local fascists took over the town, one of the most beautiful Orthodox churches was destroyed. At that time, I imagine, Ferhadija might have been afraid that its own days were numbered. Fortunately, it survived the war and the postwar years.

Ferhadija showed the first signs of poor health in 1969, when it was shaken by a powerful earthquake. It was wounded. By this time, though, the citizens of Banja Luka had realized that it was not just a mosque. They knew that it was the very soul of the city. And they did everything to heal the soul, and thus the city. They succeeded, and Banja Luka began to develop into a modern town, the centre of northern Bosnia.

I was born in 1975. When I was in second grade I had my first close encounter with Ferhadija. My class went on a field trip, and our final destination was Ferhadija. I did not know much about the arts at the time, but I remember being truly amazed by its size and shape. I had never seen anything like it before. Some things I did not understand though. For example, why would anyone take his shoes off in a public place? Nevertheless, Ferhadija's soaring height overwhelmed me, and I left with the impression that it was touching the moon. Strangely enough, another 'date' with Ferhadija was also linked with the moon.

I was taking a physics test when a Muslim priest started the call for prayer from the top of its slender minaret. Ferhadija was quite near my school. The sound disrupted my concentration. I was unable to solve a simple problem concerning the moon's gravity. I was really annoyed at the time. But now I forgive Ferhadija. Besides, it gave me a good excuse for not doing well in a test for which I was not prepared anyway.

With time, Ferhadija and I became close friends. I remember the hot summer days when thirst was almost impossible to quench. Ferhadija would always let me drink the cool water from its fountain. I remember when I sat on my balcony and looked out at the city, it was always there, the first to say 'Hello' to me. I felt that it would have done anything to make me happy.

But then people changed. There was anarchy all over Bosnia. I ran away. Ferhadija stayed behind to deal with a new kind of people. A different kind of people. They did not care for anything or anyone but themselves. They did not care for the city. And its soul, Ferhadija, was bound to realize that. *It* was breaking apart. It was slowly dying.

That day in May, first its soul and then the city itself were finished. The name of the town can still be heard. It is still on the map. But, without its soul, it is only a ghost. I know I would do anything to help people overcome that ghost. But I am not sure I will ever be able to live there again. The ghost might be overcome, the town might be rebuilt, the good old people might come back. Still, I could not bear not to see my old friend saying 'Hello' to me, when I stepped out onto my balcony to look at the city. Or maybe I could. People are strange.

D. V.
Emmett, Idaho, USA

Maybe Because I Am the Child
of a Mixed Marriage

Until the beginning of 1992 I had lived quite a normal lifestyle, like any other young person in the West. Several hours a day in the library, studying; part-time jobs; outings, parties, girlfriends. And then suddenly everything changed: barricades in the streets, tension between people. I could not believe what was happening. War was on our doorstep.

The disaster which struck my city, and the whole country, has been well covered by the international media. But there should be no limitations to revealing the truth about the people who brought misery to what was once a beautiful country. There has been an enormous number of reports from the country, but only we who lived there really know what it was like, and what it looks like now after the disaster.

From the very beginning the situation got out of control. Although the peace demonstrations, which drew thousands and thousands of people to the city's square, were meant to be a peaceful protest against warmongers, they were brutally broken up by snipers. I took part in those demonstrations demanding peace. I was still full of hope. But the first mortar attacks on the city left me astonished and in despair. I felt as if all the values I had been brought up with were disappearing. Power was in the hands of people with weapons, and the voices of ordinary, normal people were subdued by the sound of their guns.

Maybe because I am the child of a mixed marriage (my father is a Croat, my mother a Serb), it was impossible for me to accept the fact that people had started making ethnic divisions not only on the ground (the town was suddenly divided into 'Muslim' and 'Serb' parts), but also in their heads. Members of my family are of all nationalities, and for me 'ethnic background' has never been of any significance. Consequently, I thought that the current trend of growing violent nationalism was a wave of insanity.

Faced with the demand to join one armed side and then shoot at the other, which was in itself insane, I decided to go away. Those who resisted the orders of the warlords were swept aside as traitors anyway. After a number of traumatic experiences, I managed to reach Belgrade, where I had some relatives. But the situation there was not much better. Crime and shootings in the streets. Refugees crawling through the town in search of shelter and jobs. Insecurity and misery. And then strong political and media pressure on the Bosnians, especially on those who had done their military service, to go back home and fight. I spent a few weeks waiting for some miracle to stop this madness, trying to survive on the money I had left. The miracle did not happen, and my money was running out. One day, while wandering in the streets of Belgrade, I met a friend from Sarajevo who was in the same position. He told me about a possibility to leave the country, and that he had decided to go in search of a life worth living. He gave me an idea. And since June 1992 I have been living in London.

Even though I never studied English at school, I was quite fluent in it, because I read a lot (usually books borrowed from the American Center Library), and was in touch with the language through films and rock music. However, I felt a need to improve my English, especially my writing skills, so I enrolled in a one-year course, which prepared me to face my future. Since I did not know how long I would be staying here in London, I decided to take a second chance and resume my education, which had been interrupted by the war. I passed the entrance test, and now I am a student at the School of Business, University of North London. I am happy and excited about it, because it gives me a great feeling of personal achievement in spite of the disaster which destroyed my country.

You ask me how I perceive my future.

Even now while the fighting continues in Bosnia I am thinking about a way to return home, and even here thousands of miles away I have realized that the desire to go back home will always be overpowering.

At this moment it is still unclear how things will develop. News about Bosnia is contradictory: one day the peace initiative results in a ceasefire, the next day fresh fighting breaks out. And from a refugee's point of view, the prospects of returning home depend on the situation in Bosnia.

Even though our lives, and the way we think, have dramatically changed in this war, I still believe that the future of all the peoples of the former Yugoslavia lies in mutual cooperation and respect. I share that belief with my friends here in London, who are from all parts of Yugoslavia, and who are still in regular correspondence with their friends in Bosnia, Croatia and Serbia.

I believe in a new nation, built according to our beliefs, feelings and hopes, one which will not break up in a senseless, useless war. It will be not only a nation but also a kind of feeling, a love for our culture as a whole, not just for the Bosnian, Croatian or Serbian culture, but for its sum total, a common culture, which will include all the things we all love. I hope that one day we shall be known for the diversity of our culture; if not we, then our children and grandchildren.

Everybody knows that after the war, life will start again from scratch. New morals, new beliefs, new thoughts will emerge. But people will have to work together, side by side, to build something we can be proud of again, forgetting all the hate, fear and rage. Ordinary people are not like politicians, who think only about gaining more power. They want to live in peace, along with their next-door neighbours. That is how we lived before the war. Of course, I know that the people who have been fighting over there, who have been forced to fight for their survival, will be full of negative energy, of hatred, and of extreme anger, even if they refuse to admit it. Without help from those of us who were away while all that was happening, and who know that nothing is purely 'black' or 'white', reconciliation will be even harder to achieve. But ultimately we shall forget all the hostilities and build a new country, one which we will believe in and be proud of, a country of prosperity, human rights, and stability.

Perhaps my expectations are utopian. They seem so even to me when I think about all the present difficulties. But I do believe that sooner or later multilateral relationships will again flourish and they will bring about the economic growth of the whole region.

S. K.
London, UK

I Lived Happily

I was born in Sarajevo, Bosnia, where I lived all my life. I loved Sarajevo. No matter where I went, I always wanted to come back to it. My home, my family, my friends were in Sarajevo. I lived happily, surrounded by the people I loved and cared for. But all that changed when the war began.

The apartment where I lived was demolished by a shell. My family fled, and they now live in several countries. I do not know much about my close friends. I do not know where they are now, or whether they are still alive. Are they fighting, hiding, or just trying to survive? However, I do know that some of them have been killed as soldiers or civilians.

The war which struck my town is one of the worst in history. And one of the saddest. It is a war where present enemies are former friends, even members of the same family. People kill one another because of their nationality and religion, and nothing else matters to them. And this is all happening in a city where 50 per cent of all marriages are 'mixed', so that husband and wife belong to different religions or ethnic groups, and therefore to different warring sides. That's why I really don't understand the purpose of this war with so many victims.

I was raised to judge people for what they are and what they do, as individuals, not as members of religious or ethnic groups. I was raised to respect all religious and ethnic groups. Even now I don't love or hate any of these groups, or any individual for being a member of one. Each group has its good guys and its bad ones. Most of my friends, like most people in Sarajevo, were raised in the same way. But during the last two years, the war's atrocities have affected them, and many of them have changed their attitudes to such basic things as relationships between people of different national backgrounds. My own way of thinking remains the same, and it will never change, I hope.

When the war started, I was an international exchange student in the USA. When I left Sarajevo I was planning to come back in a year's time, as soon as I finished school. But after the war started, I did not want to go back, not under those circumstances. Not because I would have been hungry, cold, or afraid for my life, but because I would have lived in a place which had abandoned all the essential values of life, where my views of life would have clashed with the opinions of the majority. I did not want to go back to a city I used to love, because I wanted to live in a world where people would look at me as I really am, and judge me for what I do, not as a member of a group I'm supposed to belong to. I knew that was impossible in Sarajevo today.

So the war started and I stayed in America, where I was due to finish high school. At that point I realized that I couldn't go back to Sarajevo even if I wanted to. But I also realized that I couldn't afford to live and study in America either. In the meantime, after seven months of horror, some of my relatives managed to leave Sarajevo. They did not want to take sides in the war, they did not agree with any of them, and they did not want to fight for any of them. So they came to London, and soon I joined them there.

I was lucky. The University of Leicester accepted me and waived my tuition fees for the duration of my course. I am a second-year student now, doing a BSc degree in combined studies, studying psychology and computing as a double major. (I'd love to do an MSc degree in clinical psychology, and then work in a hospital as a clinical psychologist).

I feel that Sarajevo is the only home I have ever had, and shall ever have. No matter where I am, what I do, and how long I am away, it is the place I refer to when I talk about *home*. I only hope that one day I shall be able to go back; that one day the violence there will stop, and people in Sarajevo will live happily again; that the city will not be divided. Otherwise I shall have no place to go back to. I come from a mixed marriage and I wouldn't be able to live in a divided city where different ethnic groups do not mix. More than anything else, I want to go back to Sarajevo, but not to a city divided on ethnic lines.

Of course, once the war is over, it will not be the end of Sarajevo's troubles. It will take time to repair the damage that has been done. The city will have to be rebuilt, its economy revived. But it is the people of Sarajevo who will need help most of all. There will be many with psychological traumas caused by war, with grief for those lost in the war, with fears and constant stress. They will need help. The country will need psychiatrists and psychologists to deal with their problems. And I would love to be one of them. I would love to help people there make a happy community again.

At this moment I do not know whether that is ever going to happen. But I have my happy memories of Sarajevo, as it used to be, and I shall always remember it. And I hope that one day these memories will become reality again, not just a dream about something that happened long ago and then turned to ruins forever.

I. R.
Leicester, UK

I Thought It Was a Bad Joke. I Was Wrong.

I was born in Sarajevo in 1965. My father was Jewish and my mother is a Croatian Catholic. None of this seemed of any importance a few years ago in Bosnia-Herzegovina or anywhere else in the former Yugoslavia. Maybe I was wrong. Unfortunately, now it is very important.

Friends always came to our house. We liked them not because of their religion or nationality, but because they were true friends, or at least good people. That is what my parents taught me, and what I still believe in.

I studied civil engineering at Sarajevo University. Those were the most wonderful years of my life. We had to work hard, but we still lived an easy life, enjoying ourselves. No one ever thought about who was who, at least not the way they do now. A year before the war started, nationalists began to spread their poison among ordinary people, inciting Serbs against Croats, Muslims against Serbs, Serbs against Muslims, Croats against Serbs, and so on. People began to question their friendships and to suspect their friends. And suddenly everything changed. Even student life changed. An uneasiness and mistrust was present even among the young. Some students joined nationalist parties. I was among those who did not want to take sides, trying to strike a balance, carefully avoiding insulting anyone. We believed that everything would stop soon. I even thought that it was normal for a young democracy to have growing pains. But I misjudged the seriousness of the situation. One day a friend of mine came and warned me: 'Listen, Sarajevo is going to burn. Get out while there is still time. Take only the bare necessities, sell the rest, and go...'

That was March 1992. I was in my final year. And I simply could not take it seriously. I thought it was a bad joke. But I was wrong. What happened in Sarajevo was far worse than anyone could have predicted. I stayed in town with my mother. She did not want to leave either. We hoped that it would all soon stop. But every day Sarajevo was being bombarded more and more heavily, sometimes with thousands of different kinds of shells. The windows of our apartment were gone after only a few days. Probably because our apartment overlooked the barracks of the former Yugoslav army, we soon found ourselves on some sort of front line, between the two warring sides.

The war raged on. And as always, civilians suffered the most. Former friends took guns and pointed them at each other, neither side knowing precisely what they were fighting for. All they knew was that they should be afraid of the 'others', shoot at them, and kill them, before being killed themselves. And they expected everyone to be on their side. The pressure grew. No one could stay on the sidelines. Being a member of Sarajevo's Jewish community, I decided to take part in organizing humanitarian aid, and thus avoid conflicts with either of the warring sides. Together with a few friends of the same age, I helped deliver food and medicines to old people's homes. It was risky, because the city was under constant sniper-fire and shelling. Still, I preferred that to being directly involved in the fighting, which seemed senseless.

I wanted to leave Sarajevo, but it was not easy. I could not get a permit to leave, because I was eligible for the draft. To try to leave without the permission of the Bosnian authorities would mean to risk one's life. So I waited, carrying on with my voluntary work with the Jewish community. On 1 August 1992, my mother and I left town in a convoy organized by the Jewish community. We went through dozens of barricades, controlled by different armies, until we finally reached Split, Croatia. I left my home town as an army deserter.

In spite of the Zagreb Jewish community's efforts, we could not stay in Croatia for long. We were considered foreigners. Yet I feared I would be drafted into the Croatian army and sent back to Bosnia to fight.

Since I could not stay in Zagreb, I went to Budapest, and from there to Belgrade, and then to Titograd, Montenegro, in an attempt to complete my degree in civil engineering. The streets of Titograd (now Podgorica) were full of military police. Identification checks, questioning, deportation of young men to the front—these were all everyday scenes. And again I feared being drafted and sent to Bosnia, this time to fight with the Serbs. There seemed to be no place in Yugoslavia for me to live without fear and threats. So I kept running.

I have never been involved in any political movement, and yet I had to go into exile. Sadly, my homeland does not exist any more. It has been divided into different, ethnically cleansed regions by warring factions poisoned with hatred. I cannot identify with any of them. And it is difficult for me even to imagine going back to any of those impossible countries. In November 1992 I applied for asylum in the United Kingdom.

_N. M._
Edinburgh, UK

I Shall Do Anything to Be With Ljiljana

My father was a Serb, my mother a Muslim. For as long as I can remember, they declared themselves to be Yugoslavs. I myself prefer not to be considered a member of any of the world's tribes. My heart is there, in what used to be Yugoslavia. But it does not beat for Serbs, Muslims, Croats, not even for Yugoslavs. Not a very popular view over there these days.

I travelled throughout the former Yugoslavia and loved every part of it. My fiancée is a Croat, and now lives in Croatia. My father's family suffered a lot at the hands of Croats in the Second World War. The other half of my family is Muslim, and now they suffer at the hands of Serbs. Even if there was a good party in this war, how could I take sides?

Each side in Bosnia wants as many men in their army as they can get hold of, regardless of whether one wants to fight or not. Since I didn't want to fight, I had no choice but to run away. So I did. Twice. First I thought I had escaped when I got to Serbia. But there I had to keep my mouth shut all the time, constantly looking over my shoulder for men hunting Bosnians wanted by the army. Besides, staying there would have meant losing my fiancée for ever. And I love her very much, you see. So I had to flee.

Eventually I came to London to continue my education. I did it for a selfish reason: to secure a future for myself, wherever I end up. I guess there will always be a job for a mathematician somewhere. Since I had already completed two years in Belgrade, I thought it would be the sensible thing to do: to try to continue my schooling. Of course, there is also my love of science, but at the moment this is overshadowed by the distressing touch of poverty. This may come as a suprise to you, but I am afraid I am a very poor man right now.

So, how do I perceive my future and the possibility of returning home after I finish my studies?

What is supposed to be my home? Well, any of those lands, I suppose, provided they accept me without endangering my life. Sadly, however, none of them can do so at present.

To be quite honest, my main concern for the future is to get my degree, as I am not much use to anyone the way I am now. But then again, when I look at the more distant future, yes, I want to go back. That is where my heart is. And, as everyone knows, that means 'home'.

Please do not draw the wrong conclusion from the fact that I write so much about myself and so little about my country (-ies). There are too many people I care about there. And too many wonderful, painful memories. I just cannot afford to open those wounds. I believe in tolerance and human kindness. I cannot hate anyone. Or can I?

There are things I certainly do hate, and am even ready to fight against: nationalism, arrogance, intolerance, violence. I shall fight them by all means, whenever I get the chance. I shall also do anything I can, and much more, to be with my beloved Ljiljana.

S. K.
UK

I Was in Love and Happy

As I sit and write this essay about myself and my life now, I think about this same time of year some two years ago. My thoughts are confused and it requires an effort on my part to give them form and write them down.

So much of what has happened to me since that April, in 1992, is inconceivable, inexplicable. Until then, my only worries had been my exams, and some trifling problems in my love life. It was spring, and I was in love and happy. Everything seemed so easy and clear... And then suddenly...a nightmare started, from which I have not yet woken up.

The town where I had been studying turned into a huge cage where people were tormented in every imaginable, and soon in every unimaginable way. Many people tried to get out, but failed. I was afraid of what was happening, particularly of the hatred which was everywhere. I did not want to hate or be hated. I wanted to live, love, and dream the way I used to. 'Why,' I kept asking myself, 'is all this happening when we all used to live together in peace, wanting the same things?' Neither Sarajevo, where I studied, nor Tuzla, where I was born, were 'mine' any more. I could not call them 'mine' when they were ruled by the sick ambitions of sick people, who claimed to be fighting for my happiness and prosperity.

Fortunately, I managed to escape from Sarajevo and came to Vienna. But I escaped only physically. The war, which I have never called mine, follows me everywhere. All this time my thoughts have been back home with my family, my friends, and everything I left behind. I have never felt peace of mind.

I am determined to do my best to spend my time in Vienna usefully. But my strongest wish is to wake up from this nightmare, for the war to stop, and to see the children of my country happy and in love, as I was before that April of 1992.

Eventually I shall get a university degree. But I have already completed the school of life. I need a diploma. But I shall be truly rewarded only when I go back home, in the hope that wars like this one will never happen again. At least that is what I shall teach my children.

When will I go back home? The day that the shells stop raining down on my town. I know what I shall find there: destroyed houses, poverty, misfortune. And I know what I shall have to leave behind: the luxuries of beloved Vienna, the friends I have made here. But all the same, I shall return, to continue from where I was interrupted two years ago. It will not be easy. But I shall do my best to help my country and its people. Until then I have to use my potential to acquire knowledge, to broaden my mind through learning and to gain a better understanding of all that is new and different.

S. M.
Vienna, Austria

There Was Total Confusion

The events and their aftermath

I was born in Sarajevo in 1966 and lived there until the war in Bosnia began. It was my last year at university, exam time. I had just accepted an offer to do field research, and after graduation to start working in the Radiology Department of Kosevo Hospital, in Sarajevo. So I worked even harder than before, studying for one of my last exams, which was scheduled for 10 April.

It was 6 April 1992. The city was suddenly blocked off and became unusually quiet. The TV and radio were broadcasting conflicting reports about what was going on. We phoned our friends and relatives in other parts of Bosnia. Some of them were about to leave their homes in fear. Then the shooting started in the surrounding hills. There was total confusion. Frightened like everyone else, I talked to my boyfriend and we quickly decided to leave. I took only some clothes and my books. When we got to the coach station we saw hundreds of panicking people waiting to leave. There were extra coaches heading out of town. We all thought we were leaving for just a few days. No one could have imagined that those events would mark the beginning of such a long and savage war in Bosnia.

We had some friends in Holland and decided to wait there until the situation improved. On 7 April we found ourselves in the Hague. My boyfriend began to write to different companies, applying for jobs. I was studying for my exams, hoping to be back before the next examination period. We listened to the news every day, and could not believe the TV pictures we saw. Stupidly enough, we had not even used the word 'war' to describe events in our country. We kept talking about 'conflicts', 'disputes'… It was too hard to believe there was really a war going on there.

As the situation became more and more complicated, I decided to continue my studies in Holland. Since my financial situation was not good, I was unable to cover all the costs that this entailed, and so had to postpone my studies until the following year. I spent the intervening time working as a babysitter, saving money and trying to learn some Dutch.

In April 1993 I took a Dutch course organized by the University of Delft for foreign students hoping to enrol there. I passed the final exam and in September 1993 registered as a full-time student in the

Department of Technical Physics. They acknowledged most of the courses I had done at the University of Sarajevo, but due to the differences in the curriculum I was admitted as a third-year student. I have already passed several exams and attended a few fourth-year courses. My plan is to complete the course work and final research paper by the end of 1995.

How do I feel about it all?

Sarajevo is where I was born, the town of my childhood, which was a happy one. I lived for twenty-five peaceful years in Sarajevo, including my unforgettable school-days and life with friends and family. All that was brought to an abrupt end by a senseless war. But that cannot be the end of my life in my home town and in my country.

We knew that we belonged to different ethnic and religious groups, but there were no divisions between us, no hatred among us. We lived together happily, and never thought that it should be any different. And we were Serbs, Croats, Muslims, Jews and others, particularly the many offspring of so-called mixed marriages, like myself. We all shared our youth, our interests, problems, passions, often without even knowing each other's nationality or religion.

I still feel the same. I do not hate anyone. But I do feel an endless sorrow because hatred has overpowered love. I ask myself who really needed this unwinnable war. All the warring sides will be losers.

It is as if the forces of darkness have conquered my town and my country, bringing with them some very strange, peculiar people, whose mad ideas have caused these tragic events. We—I mean us, normal people—are needed there to restore sanity. In the meantime, we live our lives on two tracks: one here in Europe, striving to continue our education and survive, and the other there, thinking constantly of our cities, relatives, friends.

To a casual observer my life here looks as normal as anybody else's. I live with my boyfriend, we have our friends and we speak Dutch. However, our lives are much harder than those of our Dutch counterparts, because we work harder so as to suppress our pain and our despair. To us leisure means watching the news in the hope that peace will come, writing letters to our families, or reading letters from Sarajevo, with all their despair and tragic news.

But we hope that this will not last forever. And then one day we'll go back to help rebuild our country and bring love instead of hate, order instead of chaos, democracy and prosperity instead of death.

A. B.
The Hague, Holland

Chapter 2: **Out of Sarajevo**

How It Was in the Beginning

When the war started in my country I wasn't even aware of it. I was in my last year as a student of comparative literature, preparing for my finals. At first the war was merely a hindrance because it deprived me of access to the books I needed, since all the libraries in town were closed. That's how it was in the beginning.

There was the difficulty of getting books, but an even bigger problem for me was finding my friends, many of whom disappeared overnight, left, fled. I'm sure I'll run into some of them again somewhere, sometime. But gone forever are those who went to their death, and those who joined the collective madness and went to war against their own city. When I was in Sarajevo I thought I would never be able to forgive those who had fled the city when it needed them so badly. Today I don't know if I'll be able to forgive even myself for leaving. But, there it is, my generation has scattered all over the world and now we're without a country, without friends, without family. Why? Everyday life in our city suddenly became defined by the word *no*: no school, no university, no books; no water, no food, no electricity, no gas; no this, no that…

At first I was full of superhuman hope and faith in the people of Sarajevo, in their mutual respect, in the multireligious and multinational being of the city. I haven't really lost that faith to this day. But the most important thing to me at the time was to finish my senior thesis as quickly as I could, and that preoccupied me for the first two or three months of the war. Even when the shelling was so bad that we had to run down to the cellar, the first thing I thought of was saving my papers and books. I graduated on 3 July 1992 in Professor Tvrtko Kulenović's dining room, because the university building was closed and inaccessible. I was the first student to graduate (with honours) in wartime Sarajevo.

Two days later I started working with a group of Sarajevo intellectuals and enthusiasts in an extraordinary humanitarian organization called the First Children's Embassy. It has already saved thousands of Sarajevan children from hunger, death and injury. Even when the blockade of Sarajevo was at its worst, it managed to get essential medicine and food to the city's children. I worked for the Children's Embassy day and night for a full six months, without a day off (in wartime, of course, weekends and holidays don't exist). I co-edited the book *Mummy, I don't want to go to the cellar*, a collection of wartime stories written by children. Working in the Children's Embassy meant the world to us. We felt useful, we wanted to help make life a little easier for the youngest, the most innocent, the most harmless of our citizens—the children. Every day we would visit them all over the city, stage plays for them, exhibitions, poetry readings; organize playrooms and schools in cellars. I wasn't, and I didn't want to be, a soldier or a fighter. But I did want to fight for the children, against the spectre of war and the explosion of rampant nationalism.

Much of my time at the Children's Embassy was spent organizing a convoy to take 350 children and their mothers out of Sarajevo to the Czech Republic. After lengthy preparations and repeated delays, the convoy finally left Sarajevo and I left with it as group leader. For me it was a painful, wrenching experience. It's impossible to describe the pain you feel when you leave—maybe forever—your home town, familiar streets, parks, memories, loved ones. My parting kisses and goodbyes to my father—pain, pain, pain. There's no other word. And since then, there has been just more pain, worry, fear, anxiety. Today, more than a year later, that same pain is still inside me, maybe more so than before, because now I'm more aware of the distance that separates me from the world of my childhood. But because of that pain, and because of the suffering of the Sarajevans and my people, I have a burning desire to continue my education and, once the right conditions exist, to be of practical assistance, as an expert and an artist, to my city.

During the war, Sarajevo was the cultural centre of the world, especially in theatre, painting and poetry. The conditions for survival were few and far between because Sarajevans no longer had the basic requirements for life. But out of all that misery was born art of the highest quality. Plays were staged in destroyed theatre buildings, and instead of tickets people brought candles. Literary evenings and exhibitions were held by candlelight. Art outlived the war, becoming more important to Sarajevans than anything else. It was their food and water, their faith and hope. And the day that freedom and peace return, life will come back to the city and art will help Sarajevo to recover from the war. I hope to be there on that day, sufficiently well-educated to be part of that reconstruction project.

V. M.

Prague, Czech Republic

Why?

When the war started in Slovenia, my friends and I never dreamed it would spread, in a much worse form, to Bosnia-Herzegovina. We didn't think our city could fall victim to any kind of national conflict, because it was a place where young people of all nationalities lived together, where no one cared about nationality, religion or politics.

My first disappointment came when I realized that a week or two before the fighting began some people had left the city without even saying goodbye to their friends. They left in a sneaky, treacherous way, knowing exactly what was going to happen, but not even trying to warn their friends.

In April, when it was already obvious that the war had begun in Bosnia, we still thought it must be some kind of mistake and would soon be over. We hoped for military intervention which would somehow miraculously restore the nice quiet life we had led until a year before. But time dashed all our hopes, and all we were left with was disappointment.

At the very beginning, my sister and I, both of us still full of ideals and the desire to do something, signed up with our local civil defence office. But the only thing we were given to do during the several months we spent in Sarajevo was to take a population census and hand out relief aid cards. As time passed, the situation in the town grew worse and we watched the people and the city undergo terrible changes. There was only one law, the law of guns. Gangs roamed the city. I couldn't take it. My desire to leave was the natural result of everything that had happened. My parents couldn't bear it any more, knowing that I was walking around town while the sirens were sounding the alert and shells were showering the city. But I simply couldn't sit at home twiddling my thumbs. As early as July we started thinking about the coming harsh winter, about the rapidly dwindling stocks of food, about the downed power lines, and other more or less important things. We decided that my sister and I should leave the city and spend the winter with friends on the coast. When the opportunity to leave on a Jewish convoy arose, we took it.

Everything that subsequently happened was just a logical continuation of it all. When we arrived in Croatia and started thinking realistically, I realized that this war was going to go on for a long, long time. We were in Croatia almost illegally (it wasn't taking in refugees at the time), and we had no right to do anything there. There was no way for us to continue our education or do anything else. The only thing I could do was join a group of Jews going to Israel. From the beginning I decided that I would study there at Tehnion, which I had read about in a popular science journal. I needed a goal, something to fight for, and I found it in my studies. That's all I've got left from my former life.

The moment I decided to leave Sarajevo, my plans for the future changed from one day to the next. For the time being my only plan is to finish school.

When I first came to Israel I thought a lot about returning home. Everything I care most about is there.

Occasionally, I get letters from girlfriends in Sarajevo about what's happening there. They tell me not to return, that it's hell there, a hell they've all more or less grown used to. They say I'm lucky not to be there. But they don't realize something. Those of us who departed, leaving everything behind—our parents, our friends, our memories, our favourite spots and streets—left a part of ourselves behind as well. Now we're broken people trying to live new lives, to make up for what we are missing. But it's not easy and often I think it's impossible. That is why we would gladly take any opportunity to be useful, to put the pieces of our shattered lives back together again.

I don't know whether we shall ever be able to go back and live there. Only time can tell. Meanwhile, the only thing we can do for our country is to learn, and keep learning, and to forgive.

L. L.
Jerusalem, Israel

All My Future Plans Were There

I was born in Sarajevo, where I had lived all my life, except for two years with my parents in Karachi, Pakistan. I finished six grades of primary school, four grades of secondary school, and one year of university in Sarajevo. I was in my first year of dentistry at the University of Sarajevo when the war broke out.

In the months preceding the war life was pretty normal for me. I was still going to college. I was still living with my family. I was still seeing all my friends and going out as usual. The only thing which was different that spring was that I had to buckle down and study, as my exams were coming up in April. By that time I had passed biology and was studying for my physics and chemistry exams. But by the last week of March most of my friends had stopped going out as often as they used to. One could see that there were fewer and fewer things in the shops and street markets. Professors at the university were more worried than ever. My parents were strangely anxious about things that were being said. A peculiar pressure could be felt in the air. I remember that my chemistry exam, probably the most difficult in the first year, was scheduled for 8 April, and I was studying like mad.

The weekend of 4 and 5 April coincided with the last days of Ramadan, and Muslims were celebrating their holiday. But, unlike previous years, there was a lot of shooting around town. On the night of 5 April, the city was blockaded and cut off from the rest of the world. Like every Monday, the next morning I went to the university, but I found an official announcement that there would be no lectures until further notice. That was the last time I went to my university. That morning and the rest of the day a lot of shooting could be heard all around town. But, unlike the previous days, it was not from far away. I realized that it was getting closer and closer by the minute. That Monday was the last time I went out until the day I left town. My parents were still going to work, even though there was no work to be done. They did not let me go out because they felt the streets were unsafe. They were right. I spent most of my time studying, since I was sure that things would soon calm down and I would be able to take my exams. But the university didn't reopen, and lectures were cancelled for another ten days. The situation was getting worse each day.

One morning my parents told me they thought it would be better if I left for a while, at least until things settled down. At first I did not understand, but when my father said that they could not guarantee my safety, and that it would only be for a few days, like a holiday, I agreed. On 14 April I left the city with a close friend in one of the planes being used by the Yugoslav People's Army to evacuate civilians from the besieged town. I was still sure that I would soon be back and would take my exams in time, so I packed my books and took them with me.

I spent the next six months with my mother's relatives in Slovenia: with no prospects, no money, no job, no plans, no hope. That first week I was worried, but I did not yet realize how serious the situation was. I kept on reading and studying for my exams. But after a while I got depressed because it dawned on me that I was stuck in an impossible situation, with no way out. I had no chance of going back home, and I was in a country which used to be part of my homeland, Yugoslavia, but which did not want to have anything to do with people from other 'left-over' parts. For me and my friend from Sarajevo the situation was getting worse and worse, and we had to think of a way to go on with our lives without help from our family or country. After six months of despair, we set off to start a new life. My uncle bought two tickets and sent us to London, where we have now been for a year and a half.

Even if I wanted to, I would probably find it hard to explain that I left my home town, my family, and my friends, only because I thought it would be for a short while, until things settled down. And it would be even more difficult to explain that I would never have left, had I had the chance to choose, even if I had known that things would go this far and get this ugly. I love Sarajevo more than any other place in the world. All my friends, except for the one who has been with me all this time, are still there. My family and my boyfriend are still there. I felt so helpless for such a long time. But now that I have found a path to follow, continuing my studies, I feel as if my life has regained some of its purpose. As I lived most of my time in Sarajevo, everything I did was, and still is, connected with that town; all my future plans were linked to Sarajevo. A lot of things have changed there since I left. From what I have been told by my parents and friends, people have changed as well. And I feel guilty that I have not been there to see things happening, to witness these crucial historical moments of this city which I call 'mine'.

I remember that when I lived in Sarajevo I had no idea what nationality the people around me were. I still don't know, because I don't want to know. I consider this world a place of equal rights for everybody, regardless of nationality, colour, race, or origin. And I am sure that most of my friends feel as I do. I wish I could say the same for the rest of the people living in Bosnia-Herzegovina at the moment.

M. M.
London, UK

My Body, Ice-Cold With Terror

It was a year and a half ago that the first shell exploded in my native town Sarajevo, turning the coherent, happy lives of its citizens into a nightmare, into a living hell. I was living with my parents and sister at the time, and was already making great plans for my future, including finishing the last two years of high school in the United States in order to perfect my English and learn about a different culture. Nothing else, I thought, besides my ambition, devotion, and thirst for knowledge, was needed to carry out these plans and provide me with a smooth, successful life. I did not allow the war to influence me very much. In fact, I could not believe that it was real, and pretended that it was only a bad dream which would soon be over. But then a frightful incident awakened me to reality.

One night, a group of agitated armed men came to our neighbourhood looking for anybody suspicious. To be safer in case of shooting, my sister and I lay down on the living-room floor, in complete darkness and silence, hearing the occasional shouts, threats, and window-breaking that froze the blood in our veins. In the darkness my imagination ran riot with pictures of death, molestation, blood and pain. My body shook uncontrollably, ice-cold with terror, my stomach contracted in spasms, my chin trembled so much that I could not keep my teeth from chattering. Fear, like poison, entered my bloodstream—how precious one's life seems when one is in danger of losing it!

Shortly after the incident, I grabbed the opportunity to leave town in a convoy, taking with me only a suitcase with the bare necessities. When I reached the United States at the end of the summer and moved in with my aunt, I was relieved to be finally safe from snipers and shells. That, however, was not my ultimate goal, it was simply a door which opened up new challenges for me. What I was most concerned about was the continuation of my education.

Learning gives me motivation and satisfaction, and also provides me with a basis on which to build my future, starting from nothing but my knowledge and initiative. I sincerely hope you will assist me in my striving for a new beginning, because not only would it be of benefit to me personally, it would also produce one more educated person to help put an annihilated country back on its feet again.

M. T.
Beaumont, Texas, USA

Fresh Water and Food Were Luxuries

My name is A. S. I am from Bosnia, from Sarajevo. I am writing this letter desperately hoping that someone can find a way to help me.

In primary, and later in secondary school, which I attended in Sarajevo, I was always among the best pupils. In primary school my grade average was 4.0 every year, which placed me among the five best students of my class. I was subsequently accepted at one of the most distinguished high schools in Sarajevo, with the maximum possible number of points. A part of my everyday life was occupied by extracurricular activities: I was a member of the literary club, I played volleyball for my school team, I played the violin in an orchestra with which I toured Europe.

The people who influenced me the most were, of course, my parents. I was linked to them by mutual love, trust and understanding. They taught me to open my heart to others, but to judge them with my mind. I learned from them that the most precious possession one can have is knowledge. It is the only possession that can never be taken away from us.

Like all young people, I had my dreams and plans for the future. I never thought anything could stop me from making them come true. But I was wrong.

I cannot remember how many books on war I had read; I thought I knew all about it. But, again I was wrong. It is impossible to understand anything until it happens to you.

One day large black clouds filled the sky, bringing horror with them. The hatred came upon us suddenly, noiselessly, overpowering people's hearts. Almost overnight my native Sarajevo became a huge graveyard. It turned into a cave of the dead, of the silent walking shadows of those waiting to die. In order not to lose my mind while sitting for hours in the darkness of the cellar, I used to recite to myself my favourite poem by Kipling: 'If you can keep your head when all around you are losing theirs…you will be a man…' It was hard to do that. I was surrounded by people who had broken all the laws of humanity. I did not see daylight for five months. Fresh water and food were luxuries. Still, for me the most dreadful thing was to watch my parents, who had dedicated their lives to the world of science, being harassed and mistreated by illiterate, malicious armed men, who were fighting for crazy ideas born out of their own primitivism.

Fortunately, in August 1992 I managed to flee the country, leaving behind my parents, my home, everything that was mine, everything that I loved. I brought with me only my knowledge, and my hope, and I started a new life in a foreign country. I have been encouraged by the knowledge that the greatness of man lies not in his ability to stand on his feet, but in his strength to get up and carry on every time he is knocked down.

I spent the last year in Cranston, Rhode Island, where I finished high school. Currently I am a freshman at the University of Bridgeport. Despite the emotional drain, I have accomplished quite a lot.

As far as my academic goals are concerned, I plan to major in economics and take history as a minor. I am interested in the connection between economic development and the distribution of power among people from different political and territorial units. My long-term goal is to become a lawyer specializing in international law.

A. S.

Bridgeport, Connecticut, USA

There Was No End to the War

When the war started in Sarajevo in April 1992 I didn't think of leaving. In a matter of days the streets were deserted and those of us who stayed behind felt somehow abandoned, and betrayed. I refused to succumb to despair, convinced that the madness and hell wouldn't last that long. Even then, in what proved to be just the initial months of the war, I believed in the need to lay the foundations for a new, more open society. Convinced of Sarajevo's cosmopolitan character and of the openness of its people, I assumed that renewal would be quick and efficient, and so would the country's subsequent inclusion in the world order. I joined the Sarajevo Society of Architects and we set about determining the scope of the destruction, collecting graphic material and evidence of the destroyed buildings, and publishing a magazine called *War-chitecture*, which not only registered the actual situation but was also an appeal, if not for help then at least for understanding. The world seemed so cruelly indifferent, merely because normal life went on (still!) outside our borders. It was important for us to feel that we weren't forgotten, and that, despite the shelling, which was so frequent in Sarajevo it became like rain in England, we were still human beings worthy not only of compassion but also of respect. (I think I could write reams about the wonderful courage of Sarajevans, about their pride and defiance, about their city, but that, I'm afraid, is not the subject of this essay.)

In short: what I believed in then (and still believe in now) is best expressed in an article I wrote in the summer of 1992, printed in the June 1993 issue of *War-chitecture*.

However, things went from bad to worse, and instead of a short three-month war, it became increasingly evident that the end was still far off. Life imposes its own demands: there was less and less food, I had to look for a job to provide the essentials for my family. Relying on my knowledge of English, in September 1992 I applied for and got a job with UNPROFOR, Sarajevo HQ. The job permitted me to alleviate, if only for a bit of the day, the sometimes unbearable and always cruel daily hardships of life for my family, many friends and relatives. Paradoxical though it may sound, I never felt more fulfilled and useful than then. The work was never just milk and honey, of course. Because of my mixed origins (father—Muslim, mother—Serb), I was one of the few interpreters ready to cross between the warring sides. I worked mostly on 'outdoor' missions, which included everything from repairs of electricity, water and gas supplies, negotiations with the commanders on both sides and prisoner exchanges, to exchanging the bodies of killed soldiers and civilians. Sometimes it meant working in temperatures of -20° C, and often it meant being exposed to direct shelling and sniper fire. I was living through all the things I had once watched in partisan movies. Since I had no previous military education, and that was more than necessary for my job, I learned as I went along, giving the best of myself: I was personally commended for my work by General Cot, the commander of UNPROFOR for the former Yugoslavia, and Colonel Dubrug, head of UNPROFOR, Sarajevo HQ.

Then came the autumn of 1993 and I felt I couldn't take it any more. There was no end to the war in sight and I had started being afraid. Shells aren't the only things that kill in Sarajevo—fear kills as well! It paralyses you and stops you from reacting properly. That's when I decided to leave. Because I could leave. I was one of the lucky ones who had a place on a UNPROFOR plane. Other people in the city were condemned to four hours of electricity in five months, one hour of running water in half a year, warming themselves over a tin which by some miracle becomes a stove. Believe me, it isn't easy to leave Sarajevo. If you have ever had to leave a sick, helpless child, then you will know the feeling!

The only thing that keeps me going is my faith: I firmly believe that one day, when all this is over, my country, my city and my people will need strong, educated people to rebuild everything, not just buildings, but also shattered hopes and the will to live. Where I come from, people believe that hope is the last thing to die.

Since I'm not there, where I should be, I shall use this time to make myself more prepared and useful for the future which is bound to come one day. That's what I learned in Greek tragedies. I think I am closer to catharsis now...

Sarajevo was shelled again today.

We're a step further from peace again.

We have to travel again.

We have to cross the river...

I. A.

London, UK

I Had Had Enough

I worked as a journalist from the age of eighteen, while studying at the University of Sarajevo. When it became clear that there was going to be war in Bosnia-Herzegovina, Worldwide Television News (WTN) opened an office in Sarajevo, and I was chosen to work with them. My duties included supervision of the crew, feeding material through to London, field production and translation. Later I became a coordinator for the pool office which shot TV material for a range of broadcasting companies, including American and British networks and the Eurovision exchange. I acted as liaison between the UN, foreign TV crews and the local people, including the Bosnian government.

I don't want to write about my personal war experience, because I am sure you have enough information about the situation in Sarajevo. Suffice it to say that I left Sarajevo on 1 August 1993, after sixteen months of horror. The pressure became too much. Even before the war in Bosnia, I had covered the Croatian conflict, and at a certain point I had had enough.

Because of my work with the world media I was among the few privileged Sarajevans who could travel in wartime. Before I fled from Sarajevo, I had already been out of the city on several occasions, once even for a short holiday. One day, when I felt outraged by events, I finally decided to leave. When I say 'finally', I mean that I decided not to come back until the war was over. I was so oppressed by the experience of war. Now, however, I feel homesick. It is my intention to go back as soon as I've finished my studies.

E. B.
London, UK

The Most Wonderful Thing Happened to Me

I was born in Sarajevo, Bosnia-Herzegovina. For as long as I can remember, I wanted to be a doctor. I finished primary school in Sarajevo, and secondary school in Baghdad, where I lived with my parents for five years. When I returned to Sarajevo, I enrolled at the Medical School of Sarajevo University. I completed four years and passed twenty-five exams. My husband and I lived in a part of Sarajevo which was occupied by the aggressor. We had to abandon our apartment under very dramatic circumstances, simply to save our lives. We left all our possessions, our clothes, our documents, all the small but important necessities of life. Our apartment was looted and burned down. My husband and I became refugees in our own city.

Sarajevo's Central Hospital appealed for people to help the struggling teams of doctors. I volunteered. I spent the first weeks of the war working in the hospital twenty-four hours a day. The war went on, but my school continued with classes and exams, and I attended regularly. In January 1993 I became pregnant but I continued to work both at school and at the hospital. Most of my time was spent with wounded children. On 6 October 1993 I gave birth to a healthy baby. The most wonderful thing had happened to me in the middle of this monstrous war. Ten days after I left the hospital with my baby, my parents' house, where we all lived, was hit four times by shells, and was demolished. Winter was coming, and we did not have a roof over our heads. For the second time, now with a small baby, we felt the despair of war. My husband, who is a professional athlete, contacted friends of his in France, who helped us to come here as refugees. We had to leave Sarajevo for the sake of our baby.

After we came to France, it took us a long time to get used to normal life. Street lights, TV, running water, showers—everything was a miracle to us. We had been living without these everyday things for two years. Each day I thought about the hell I had been living in, and realized that I had been happy there, being able to help injured children, which is an unusual position for medical students. Then I decided to finish my studies, so that I could go on helping wounded children and the sick. My greatest wish is for peace to return to Bosnia; *peace*, such a common word, but so magical, so precious, for without it a human being loses everything, absolutely everything. I hope that democracy, respect for differences and tolerance among nations will lay the ground for a new country, and that the awful things caused by war will never be repeated.

A. N.
Paris, France

The Decision to Leave Sarajevo Was One of the Hardest of My Life

My decision to leave Sarajevo and Bosnia-Herzegovina temporarily at the end of September 1993 was one of the hardest of my life. Sarajevo was, still is, and in my firm conviction will remain, one of the most beautiful, sensitive, artistically attractive and historically interesting places this planet has to offer.

I see myself now and in the future as an active participant in the city's life, contributing to its culture and sharing its future.

Sarajevo is a magical place, a city where different approaches to life and death converge, interact and blend. This peculiar sensibility was clearly evident in the years before the war. Sarajevo was one of the most influential centres of cultural innovation in Yugoslavia. It was home to the International Days of Poetry; the Yugoslav Documenta, an annual art exhibition; the International Festival of Fringe and Experimental Theatre; the Obala Open Stage; the Sarajevo Film School (Emir Kusturica, Ademir Kenović); and even hosted the 1984 Winter Olympic Games. Because of this sensibility developed over the decades, the continuing siege of Sarajevo has failed to kill the city's spiritual life.

As the Open Society Fund already knows, and has proven by establishing a foundation in the capital of Bosnia-Herzegovina, a part of Sarajevo's magic lies in its ability to offer a uniquely non-violent code of self-defence: death is counteracted with life, destruction with creativity, fear of difference with an openness reflected in centuries of multicultural coexistence. One could draw a comparison with Gandhi and his struggle for his country's freedom, which inspired strong civil protest movements during the Cold War years.

Sarajevo is a city where the university was reopened in wartime even though all its buildings had been severely damaged by shells fired from the hills. A city where hospitals, bakeries and the brewery have remained open in spite of daily shelling. A city where, despite constant sniper-fire, theatre performances are attended as though it were peacetime. A besieged city, where young people rehearse the musical 'Hair' by candlelight, while guns from the surrounding hills bombard playgrounds. Where one of the great human souls of contemporary Europe, Vedran Smailović, played his cello in a tuxedo and white tie on the spot where a shell had landed only twenty minutes before, while people stood around, listening in silence.

Sarajevo is, I claim, a sensitive and highly civilized place. But if that is so, then you might ask: Why should one want to leave? Why did I leave after eighteen months of war?

I shall try to explain as briefly as possible:

We are living in what are—without doubt—times of great, significant change. The Cold War is officially over. The political and social structures it generated seem to have disappeared. The balance of fear, which marked the whole world, especially Europe, over the last half-century, has also disappeared. But an immense energy has been released, filling the void that was left. It is an exciting but very dangerous situation. As history teaches us, whenever it is faced with great challenges, the human race does not immediately stand up to them. The sense of victory on one side of what used to be the Iron

Curtain does not ensure a new, better world, as present events clearly demonstrate. The changes that have taken place in the countries of the former communist bloc ought to be followed up with genuine dialogue based on the idea of the open society. By that I mean that in an open society more than one system of values should prevail, without the desire of one to patronize or control others. Such a positive confrontation would be of mutual benefit to everyone involved. But it is essential that this dialogue should be conducted by open-minded people, who view differences as a positive and inspiring phenomenon. The most important part of the process is: to question. One needs to ask, to explore, to search, to seek, to demand answers. Through dialogue. Through dispute. Arguing and exchanging views. One should keep one's mind open.

At the end of the summer of 1993 I began to feel that I was no longer able to ask questions. I became too much of a 'one-way person'. And I had no doubts. Then the University of Edinburgh offered to extend my status as a non-graduating student at the Faculty of Arts for the 1993–94 session. I realized that it was the most important thing to happen in my life. It was a chance to join a 'two-way street', through education. So I decided to leave Sarajevo in order to come back. To continue asking questions, together with my whole generation, which—with a proper education—will be able to carry on the hopes of a new society. Or should I say: with that part of my generation which survived and overcame the consequences of intolerance and war.

B. Z.

Edinburgh, UK

We Do Not Share the Same Destiny Any More

I left my native Sarajevo in May 1992, a month after the war started. I was in my final year of high school, studying for the entrance exam to Sarajevo's Academy of Arts. No one believed what was happening. All my dreams were shattered, not only mine, but those of everyone who shared the same destiny. We felt confused, lost, insecure. It was the beginning of an obscene tragedy. The schools had finished two months earlier than usual. Masses of young people found themselves facing decisions they hoped they would never have to make. To stand up and fight, not for politics, but for their own homes, town, future. We had to make our choice, but whatever our decision the loss was ours. My parents were pressuring me to leave the country. They wanted me to have a chance, to continue my education, and most of all they wanted to save the life of their only child. They told me that the only hope for me was to finish my education and make something of my life. I did not want to go. All my friends were staying, some of them joined the Bosnian army. My mother is a doctor, she was hardly ever at home, spending days and nights at the hospital. I wanted her to leave with me. She wouldn't. 'It's my duty as a doctor to stay and help,' she said. 'I wouldn't be able to live with myself knowing that I'd left when they needed me most.' She is still in Sarajevo, working. I left on 19 May with a convoy for Split, Croatia. I was in complete despair, alone, without my parents, worried for their lives. But my future was in my hands. There was no way back.

I passed the entrance exam at the Academy of Arts in the Croatian capital, Zagreb. But the deteriorating situation there would have made it impossible for me to study seriously. So I decided to go to England and to try to continue my studies there. I managed to enrol at the Berkshire College of Art and Design, where I finished the preparatory studies course in art and design.

I do not think much about my past any more. I learned to survive and start a new life. It was not easy. I had lost my town, my country, my identity. I lived wondering whether I would ever see my parents again. But I had my art. Art is my weapon, my reaction, my scream against the evil of destruction that surrounds us. The only noble way to fight for a better world. And I do not think much about returning home either. I want to finish my studies first. As much as I want to go back, the idea of returning scares me. That would again be a new beginning, a painful and ruthless step that I have already made once. Besides, I wonder whether I would be able to face my friends again. A lot of them have been killed, many have been wounded, others might not understand me. We do not share the same destiny any more.

N. S.

London, UK

Chapter 3: **Experiences**

And Then the War Happened

I was born on 29 January 1976 in Jajce, Bosnia-Herzegovina, where I finished elementary school as the best student in my class. I had a happy childhood and my life was full of promise.

And then the war happened. I found myself in the middle of events which I could not have imagined in my worst nightmares. I endured seven months of horror in a dreadful war. Seven months without food, water, electricity… Every day I saw people dying. Some from shells, some from snipers, some from bombs. (Sometimes aeroplanes bombed the town four times a day.) I don't have words to describe what it was like.

By the end of August everyone knew that the town would fall into the hands of the Serbs. Our defences were becoming weaker and weaker by the day, and the circle around the town kept tightening. It was as if we were in an arena, waiting to be killed. Panic overwhelmed the town. People expected someone or something to help them, but in vain. That someone or something never appeared. I had friends who could not stand the pressure and killed themselves.

Then on 17 October 1992 an evacuation was announced—across Mount Vlasić. I could do it, but not my parents. Since I was afraid to walk across the mountain by myself, my mother accompanied me. For twenty-four hours we walked through roadless highlands, under gunfire the whole time. For twenty-four hours we were targets for Serbian artillery. Our convoy stopped in Travnik, where I had to say goodbye to my mother and go on alone. She returned to my father. Twelve days later Jajce fell. My parents are now refugees in Zenica. There is hunger in Zenica, but I hope they will survive.

After fleeing Bosnia, with all the indescribable troubles we Bosnian refugees had to suffer, I arrived in the Czech Republic. I have tried to resume as normal a life as possible. I attended the third grade of high school in Tisnov. To continue regular schooling I had to take third-year exams, which I passed with very good marks, and I am now in the fourth year. I finished the first term near the top of the class. I have overcome all barriers, even the language barrier.

I want to continue my education. That is the best way to help myself, my parents and my country. Bosnia will need educated people when the war stops. I have applied to Charles University in Prague. I want to study history and English; history has always been my favourite subject.

After I finish my studies I want to return to my parents and my homeland. I will try to build a new home for my parents and me, to walk through the streets and talk with my friends in my native language, to build a new society without hate or discrimination. *And I know I will!*

M. P.

Prague, Czech Republic

Hiding and Living in Fear

It all began on 3 May 1992.

I was woken up by a mobile loudspeaker saying that all Muslims and Croats had to turn in their weapons or else…

Standing on the terrace I wondered who these Muslims and Croats were and why everyone had suddenly become a Serb, Muslim or Croat, when no one had ever paid attention to such things before.

Who were these people in uniform marching in the street and what were they doing in my town?

It was like a circus, a joke, but three hours later everything became inexplicably real, with houses burning and those same soldiers shooting.

Later, among the men who expelled some twenty thousand people that day, I recognized some of the 'friends' with whom I had celebrated May Day just two days before, with whom I had talked about the harmony of life in Bosnia, something that nobody could ever destroy!

Had somebody there been naive?

I spent five months hiding in our apartment with my parents and brother, hiding and living in fear: in fear of people who called themselves Serbs and to whom I was merely somebody of a different nationality who had to be made as miserable as possible, who had to be beaten or killed.

When the Serbs started mobilizing men into their own purely national army, my parents gave their last coins to the mafia to get my brother and me to Vojvodina, where my mother's brother lived. Another night of horror, driving through destroyed northern Bosnia with false papers. Until then I had only seen this in the movies.

Soon after we reached Vojvodina, we had to decide where to go from there. It was hard, because we didn't know anyone anywhere in Europe. Germany looked the most promising. On the way there we had to change trains in Prague. We found we were at the wrong station in Prague; we didn't know there was more than one, we were lost. My brother ran into a Welshman who helped us find the main station.

Having known us for only two hours, the young Welshman offered to help us. He said that if we didn't manage to pass the German border control, we could use his apartment while he was away in Britain. It was a miracle, like a dream.

We never went to Germany, because at the train station we met people from the former Yugoslavia who had just been sent back from the border. Our only hope was to ask for the keys of the nice Welshman's apartment. We got them. After he returned (the man's name is Ereig Lewis Derby) we met lots of people. I enrolled at the university and my brother began working as a designer. We are doing what we really wanted to do.

There was another side to life, though. For my brother and me it was happy, but for our parents it was hell. It's so strange. Only 800 kilometres separate our lives.

D. L.
Prague, Czech Republic

My Parents Begged Me Not to Return

Until the summer of 1991 I was a normal Yugoslav teenager, with the same problems as most teenagers in the world. I was planning to enrol at the University of Sarajevo in September that year. I had already arranged to share a student room with one of my best friends. I was looking forward to beginning my life as a student. Then I learned that nothing in life is a hundred per cent certain.

That summer everything changed. Fighting broke out in some villages near Bihać, my home town. Only ten miles from the town, in the lake district of Plitvice, I saw burnt-out houses. I heard of people, ordinary people, being persecuted. My parents received threatening calls, and my next-door neighbour was beaten up in his own house. Tension in Bihać mounted, with people fearing for the future.

These events had a great impact on me and I decided to leave for a few months, until the situation normalized. My parents were very concerned about my safety and encouraged me to go to England, both for refuge and to improve my English. However, during my stay in England the fighting spread to the whole of Bosnia-Herzegovina. And it's still going on...

My family has suffered dreadful harassment and humiliation in this war, forcing them to leave their home and possessions and flee Bihać. Horrific brutalities were committed during the 'ethnic cleansing' process. So much so that my parents begged me not to return, because they feared for my life. They felt very strongly about it because they had had first-hand experience of constant harassment as members of a particular ethnic group. They wanted me to stay far away, even if it meant never seeing me again.

For nearly two years I hoped that the fighting would stop and that I would be able to go back home and resume my studies in Sarajevo. Unfortunately, the war shows no signs of abating. And I have been forced to make alternative plans for my future. Here in England I have the opportunity to pursue my education, and develop my interest in and knowledge of economics.

D. S.
London, UK

The Elderly and Children Could Not Run Fast Enough

In June 1988 I finished secondary school as a straight A student. In October of that year I enrolled at the Medical School of Sarajevo University. I completed my pre-clinical training. It was a promising start, and I felt great. Then in April 1992 war broke out in Sarajevo. For the first few weeks we attended lectures regularly, but as the war claimed its first victims, classes were cancelled. On 30 April I took the last train out of Sarajevo. I went to Jajce, where I joined my parents. We all thought that the war would soon stop and that we would get back to our normal lives. But the war spread like wildfire, and at the end of May we found ourselves surrounded by the Serb Army. The only way out of the besieged town was past the gunfire between the two front lines. We managed to escape by running. The elderly and children were killed because they could not run fast enough. My father was badly wounded when he tried to protect me. (Our escape was a nightmare; I want to forget it.) After fifty-two hours of marching through no man's land, across Mount Vlasić, we reached the town of Travnik, where we received first aid and were given something to eat. I was allowed to leave Bosnia, but my parents had to stay. I went to Zagreb, Croatia, where I met a family friend. She took me to Graz where she lives. Since my sister was already in England (she went there as an au pair in February 1992), I wanted to join her. I arrived in London on 21 July 1992 and applied for political asylum in November the same year. In September 1992 I started to attend an English language school to study for the First Certificate in English, and in October 1993 I enrolled at the Charing Cross and Westminster Medical School as a full-time student. I am determined to finish my studies.

S. H.
London, UK

Our House Was Repeatedly Raided

I was born on 10 April 1975 in Zvornik, a pretty little town on the left side of the River Drina, in Bosnia. I spent the first seventeen happy years of my life there. I finished primary and secondary school in Zvornik, had a lot of friends and relatives... Everything in my life was—or seemed to be—just perfect. Until...

The war. It started in Zvornik on 8 April 1992, shattering all my dreams, hopes and plans.

For the first two weeks after the Serbs occupied Zvornik we lived in the woods outside town, where thousands of people tried to find shelter. When the situation seemed to calm down, I returned to town with my family, thinking that since we were innocent civilians no one would have anything against us. But that was a mistake. We returned to our house, and lived there for a while. But we lost all our human rights, my parents lost their jobs, our house was repeatedly raided, armed men and militants kept disturbing us. We heard that some of our neighbours and friends had been killed in the camps around town. Suddenly we lost our Serb friends, because, being Muslims, we were regarded as their enemies. Two months later, the new Serb authorities gave us an ultimatum—either leave town or be taken to a detention camp. So, on 5 June 1992 we left Zvornik, and a few days later arrived in Slovenia, where we were housed in a refugee camp in Maribor.

As soon as we settled down I began enquiring about the possibilities for study in Slovenia or Croatia. I was told that I could do it, but I would be considered a foreigner, which meant that I would have to pay a lot of money, and I didn't have any.

Since I had no other option, I stayed in the camp and began to work as a translator of English. I happened to meet a Swiss journalist and told him my problems. It was from him that I learned that I could study in Austria free of charge. But I did not know German. Still I decided that the best way to learn a language was to go to the country where it is spoken. I asked the Swiss journalist if he could help me. A week or so later he wrote to say that his brother's family would like to have me while I learned German. That was how I went to Villingen, Germany, at the beginning of September 1992. I stayed with the wonderful Bucher family for about 14 months. I was lucky to meet such marvellous people. With them I improved my English (the wife is

American) and learned German without any difficulty.

In the meantime, my parents had gone to Graz, Austria. Since we wanted to be together again, I applied for admission to Graz University. Four weeks later I received notification: the answer was yes. In the autumn of 1993 I passed the German language test, and now I am a medical student at Karl Frauzes University in Graz.

My dreams have finally come true!

K. A.

Graz, Austria

You Could See Hungry People in the Streets

I used to live in Zenica, an industrial town in central Bosnia. It is seventy kilometres away from the capital city of Sarajevo, where the war started. At first it all seemed remote from us and our lives. We were astonished that such horrible things were happening in our country, but we thought there was not much to worry about, it was something far away, caused by political upheavals in the capital. However, the situation in our town began deteriorating by the day.

First, at the beginning of May 1992, all the schools were closed. The end of the school year was moved forward, and I finished my third year of high school two months earlier than scheduled. There was fear of air strikes and bombing. We heard sirens all the time. Then, the steelworks, which employed more than a half the town's population, were closed. The workers lost their jobs. My father was one of them. The situation became dreadful. There was no food and no money. Every day more and more refugees from all over the country poured into town. You could see hungry people in the streets. And very young soldiers.

The sad thing for me, my sister and my brother was that we could not go to school any more. We didn't understand what was happening. But we realized that we had better leave town. We discovered that England was the only country we could escape to at the time. It was very hard for us to make the decision to leave. But the shortage of food, water and electricity, and the fear of what tomorrow would bring made us leave. The road from Zenica over the mountains to Croatia was still open at the time. My father stayed behind, but my mother, sister, brother and I went to Croatia, and from there to London.

After we settled down, I started to go to school again. It was very hard because I didn't know any English. But the universal language of mathematics, which I was good at, helped me to communicate in school. I began to study English intensively, and then things improved considerably. I thought about my friends back in Zenica, about my father and other relatives there, and it gave me the strength to work hard and to adjust to a different way of living. Now I am in my second year at Brooklands College, where I hope to gain enough basic knowledge for my future studies. I want to study mechanical engineering.

A. L.
London, UK

We Drove Through a Hail of Bullets

The day of 4 April 1992 was like any other Friday in Sarajevo. I returned to my flat after my geometry class at the university and packed my bags to go home to Mostar for the weekend, because the next day was a Muslim feast day and I wanted to celebrate it with my family.

The train journey from Sarajevo to Mostar usually took two hours, but that day it was very slow. I was not impatient. I was just looking forward to seeing the blue skies over Mostar, to being with my family, and to tasting the first cherries from our garden. My daydreaming was suddenly interrupted by the noise of the train braking. We ground to a complete halt just six or seven kilometres outside of Mostar. When the screeching noise of the train wound down, I became aware of a much more terrifying noise outside—the sound of machine-guns. Then soldiers appeared. They jumped up onto the train fully armed and forced us to get out, saying that the train would not be allowed to go any further. Frightened, bewildered, reluctant, I took my bags and with a crowd of people set off for Mostar on foot. As we approached the town the shooting became heavier, and our fears grew. We were surrounded by soldiers, who warned us to move away from the train tracks and continue down the main road. There was shooting from both sides of the road. The soldiers told us that they couldn't guarantee our safety if we insisted on going to Mostar. But we had no choice. We couldn't go back. So I kept walking down the road. Meanwhile, my brother, who had been waiting for me at the railway station in Mostar, heard what had happened. Together with some other people who had also been waiting for friends and relatives, they came by car to fetch us. When I saw my brother in his car, I felt safe. I always felt safe with him, but this time it was different. The short ride to Mostar was hell. He drove through a hail of bullets. The shooting continued unabated as the convoy of cars tried to make its way back to town. Somehow we managed to reach Mostar. Later I heard that the shooting had started after someone had blown up the barracks in Mostar.

That was the beginning of the war for me. We spent the following nights in the cellar, and the days under sniper-fire. Mostar was being shelled from the surrounding hills. We had to black out our window with blankets, and we piled up sandbags along the walls. Every day was a struggle to get food. And every day it became more and more difficult, because supplies were dwindling and money was running out. We had no electricity any more, and we desperately tried to collect water, since we knew that the water supply was low. The telephone lines were down.

Although we were trapped in our house, we managed to get news of what was going on outside, of friends who had been killed, of houses burnt down, of convoys of women and children fleeing town. On 5 May our house was hit by a shell. The roof collapsed, the windows blew in, there was debris everywhere. My mother was desperate. She begged me to leave Mostar. I did not want to leave her (my father had died five years earlier), but in the end, for her sake, I decided to go. I packed a pair of jeans, a jacket and a couple of T-shirts. My passport and student ID were safely in my pocket. Equipped, I set out into the unknown.

I arrived in Austria on 28 June 1992 and I've been here ever since. I didn't see my mother for sixteen months. Then in October 1993 Austrian friends helped me to get her to Graz, and we were reunited, a day I shall never forget.

After attending a German course at Graz University and passing the German language test (a requirement if you want to enrol at the university), I resumed my studies in architecture. (I had done two years at the University of Sarajevo.) As far as the future is concerned, my first goal is to graduate as soon as possible. Then—and this is my greatest dream—I will return to Bosnia and help rebuild the country. Architects will be greatly needed there. If the situation allows, I shall play a part in building a new Bosnia, a Bosnia where people can live in peace and safety.

E. D.
Graz, Austria

Escape from Mostar

In September 1991 the Yugoslav Army surrounded Mostar and took up military positions around town. At first the shelling and shooting was only in the evening, increasing during the night. But from April 1992 it disrupted our days as well. My son was two years old at the time, and for his sake I left Mostar for Croatia. My husband stayed behind. But after only four months away, I decided to go back, even though Mostar was still being shelled. I was feeling less and less safe in Croatia, because some refugee families were beginning to disappear in mysterious circumstances. Once back in Mostar, I tried to return to a half-normal family life again. My husband went back to work, and my son was able to play outside when the shelling stopped. I even tried to resume my studies at the University of Mostar. And I managed to pass eight exams. But...

In the early morning of a beautiful day in May, exactly one year after the first Serbian shell had fallen on Mostar, the first Croatian shell hit the town. And the real horror began. Croatian soldiers created havoc everywhere. Muslim families were thrown out of their homes. They were hunted down and forced to move to the other side of the river. Many were arrested and disappeared. My husband had to flee and I stayed behind with my son as my maiden name was Croatian.

That was the worst moment of my life—my husband having to disappear, I didn't know where, and me staying behind with my young child.

Life had to go on. We had to be very careful and keep as low a profile as possible. There was shooting and looting all around us. I had to take care not to call my son by his Muslim name. But I was prepared to do all that, because I still hoped that there were some people left who thought like me, who believed that Mostar would not and should not be destroyed. That hope did not last long. One day a Croatian neighbour warned me that he would personally kill both me and my son if we stayed, because he knew that my son's name was Hasan. With my son's safety uppermost in my mind, I realized that the two of us would have to leave. On 21 October 1993 we managed secretly to escape from Mostar. After a long, dangerous and exhausting journey, we arrived in Graz, Austria, and reached safety, but I was worried about my husband whom I had had to leave behind and who was always in my thoughts and heart.

You will understand how difficult it is for me to talk about my studies, while remembering what happened to me and to my family in Mostar. But I had managed to continue my law studies in Mostar before the Croats arrived. I used to study in our cellar, by candlelight, while Serb artillery shelled the town. The University of Mostar was still open at the time, but it had moved to a nearby village. Even so, I managed to go and take my exams there. From September 1992 to May 1993 I passed eight exams. On 10 May I was due to take one of my hardest exams, but on the 9th Croatian soldiers stormed Mostar and my life was turned upside down.

Now that we are safe, my ambition is to complete my law studies. I am so grateful that I can do so here in Graz. And I am even more grateful that my son can now live a decent life in a safe environment. (He is three years old now and goes to kindergarten.)

As far as the future is concerned, I want to go back to Mostar, to live there with my family. I would like to be a judge, and, as such, to help reestablish the legal system in my country, so that my people will once again be able to live without fear, in a democratic society.

A. D.

Graz, Austria

I Was Badly Wounded

I am a former student from the former Yugoslavia. I was born and raised in Sarajevo. On 23 December 1992 my younger brother and I left Sarajevo with the help of MDM (Médécins du Monde). The reason was painful, distressing, terrible. On 20 July 1992 I was badly wounded. That same day, at that same spot, my father was killed. For six whole months I fought for my life and then for my recovery. By December 1992 surgeons from two Sarajevo hospitals had done their superhuman best, but they could do nothing more for me, they simply didn't have the conditions. It was essential for me to continue treatment abroad.

The opportunity to get out of the besieged city came suddenly, unexpectedly. I was put on a list of injured children due to be sent via MDM to France. I had only 22 hours from the moment I learned that I was on the list to the moment of my actual departure. You may think that wasn't time enough to make such a decision, and you may be right. Because I left everything behind: my mother, my father's grave (which I never got to visit because the cemetery was being shelled every day), all my friends, my childhood, my youth. And my future… Still, my mother, brother and I made our decision…

I had to go and get better. I had to go and give myself the chance of living a normal life. I had to go and get an artificial limb for my right arm, which had been amputated because there was no way to save it. I had to go and get an education so that one day I could be my own person and be independent. In December 1992 all that was impossible in Sarajevo. So I left, with pain in my heart and tears in my eyes. But I knew that one day I would return. That is why, here in Paris, I summoned all my strength to get better and complete my treatment. I got an artificial arm. I studied and improved my French. I enrolled at the university. Of course, I had to change my career plans. In Sarajevo I had studied architecture but I had to change that because an architect needs two hands. I found something else, something I had always had a keen interest in—philosophy. I found myself again…Today my studies mean the world to me. Some of the new things I have learned help me to understand why all of this had to happen to my country. But did it have to happen? I still don't know the answer. Does anybody? Is there an answer? Because nothing can explain the horror and misery of what is happening there. But one thing I do know. I will finish my studies. And I will go back to where my roots are, to live there and help out. Because my country needs educated people to end this war and begin anew. All over again. Only this time on the firm foundations of democracy and, above all, humanity.

B. V.
Paris, France

I Had Problems Because of My Serbian Father and Muslim Mother

I was born in 1974 in Zenica, Bosnia-Herzegovina. My father is a Serb, and my mother a Muslim. Tradition and my family name dictate that I should be of Serbian nationality, but I have always felt Yugoslav. I spent the first six years of my life in Zenica, then we moved to Karlovac, Croatia, where I finished high school. I was a good student throughout, but always had time for my hobbies: basketball and languages. I was a member of the Karlovac basketball team, which competed first in the regional and then in the national league. I was also fond of tennis, swimming and photography. I wanted to enrol at the University of Zagreb, and was looking forward to life as a student. But then the war broke out in Croatia.

Not only was I unable to continue my education because of the war, but I also had problems because of my Serbian father and Muslim mother. My entire family was persecuted. Eventually we were forced to leave and go to Belgrade, where my father's sister lived. But our troubles did not end there: my mother was Muslim, and I had a Croatian accent. Nobody wanted to talk to me. I was bullied because of my dialect. We realized that we could not stay there either. Again we had to flee. And, even worse, to separate. My father had to find a job, to support us. He went to Krajina to work for the Serb army. My mother went to Croatia to stay with relatives. I wanted to continue my studies, but since I was unable to do so anywhere in Yugoslavia, I left the country and went to France, where my sister lived. There I enrolled at the University of Le Mans. I completed a one-year certificate course in the French language. But again I had no luck. My sister and her husband got jobs in Madagascar and left France. Since I had no one in France to support me, and couldn't return to Yugoslavia, I came to England, where family friends lived. As soon as I arrived, I sought asylum. It was the first time in two years that I felt some kind of security. It made me believe that finally I would be able to start my university studies properly.

S. Z.
London, UK

They Became Refugees in Their Own Country

I am the child of a mixed marriage: my father is a Serb, my mother a Croat. I was brought up as a Yugoslav, which is what I considered myself to be. I grew up in Gunja, a small Croatian village on the border with Bosnia. I finished high school in the neighbouring Bosnian town of Brcko. Living in a multiethnic community, with Muslims, Croats and Serbs as my friends, I grew up respecting all the nationalities of the former Yugoslavia.

But in 1991, when hatred between the Serbs and the Croats started to grow in Croatia, I began to feel pressure in my immediate environment to take sides, something I did not want to and could not do. I could not identify with the increasingly aggressive nationalism of the Croats, or with the militant aggressive aspirations of the Serbs. Above all, I resented the unjustifiable idea of killing as a way to resolve social and political problems, not to mention the problems of 'national destiny'. Whatever one's beliefs and national identity, everyone has the same right to life.

In the summer of 1991 I was in Osijek, Croatia, preparing for my finals, when the first Serbian artillery shells hit town. War had broken out. Nevertheless, I managed to graduate, and spent the rest of the summer with my family in Gunja. I was waiting to go to Ilok, a little town in eastern Croatia, on the border with Serbia, where I was due to begin my teaching career. But Serb forces had already occupied the town. Two days later I fled to Germany, under pressure from my panic-stricken parents. At the time I thought I would be away a month or two. I could not really believe that an ethnic conflict would develop into full-scale war. Soon after my departure, my parents were forced to leave because of constant fighting in the region. They moved to a safer part of Croatia; they became refugees in their own country.

L. Z.
London, UK

My Father Was a Political Prisoner

I left my home town a few days before the arrival of Serb paramilitary forces. I don't remember being scared, though I must have been, otherwise I would not have fled. What I do remember is my naive belief that nothing was going to happen to my world, regardless of the armies that were at the gates of the town, regardless of who they were and what they wanted. In fact, I remember those few weeks before the war better and more vividly than anything that happened later, in the following two years. Perhaps because what happened afterwards was so awful and inexplicable that I simply don't want to remember it.

I was brought up in quite unusual circumstances. My father was a political prisoner in Yugoslavia. As a result, I was somehow aware that things in the country were not as shiny and bright as depicted to us in school and in the media. Still, I don't remember ever expecting anything bad to happen to me in Yugoslavia.

I always felt strongly about being able to express one's opinions openly, probably because I realized that that was the only crime my father had ever committed. But since I was brought up in safety, knowing the many good sides of Yugoslavia, I managed to come to terms with all its imperfections. I even blamed my father for being unable to conform to the rules of Yugoslav society, to accept them with all their constraints. This process of coming to terms with my country, and with my family inside that country, was sometimes quite painful, particularly because I was preoccupied with the business of growing up. As I grew older, I often found myself confused and inconsistent in my views and attitudes. When I was younger, for example, I felt ashamed that my father was an enemy of the state. I was only nine when he went to prison, and almost seventeen when he came home. All that time I was painfully ashamed of someone who had dared to say something 'wrong' about our ideal, flawless society. I was made to believe in that society, but I also lived in it, and I truly loved it. The only reasonable explanation I could find for my father was that he was irresponsible, mad, or extremely bad. Later, when he came home, I got to know him, and I realized that he was neither mad nor bad, and that I had been too young and 'ideologically' blind to understand him, his 'guilt', and the things happening around us. By then I had begun my studies, and I started to comprehend how society was organized. Gradually I realized that our socialist, non-aligned, self-managing system was not the best in the world, as most of us had been led to believe.

Then I went to England for a year, and that put an end to my growing pains. I finally put the pieces of the puzzle together. I remember how delighted I was with the things I found there, where people could say whatever they wanted. But I was disappointed by other things: everything seemed to revolve around money. I realized that my mental *gestalt* was the product of a completely different system of values. I preferred the 'good old' value system at home. Then I returned home, to Yugoslavia, so happy, self-assured, finally at peace with myself, with my father, with my country, with where and how I wanted to live. I really loved that country, with all its good sides and bad, with all its wonderful and awful people... I still believe that I loved the country much more than some other people who had not had the kind of problems I had in growing up there. I had invested so much in it, all my heart, and endless hours of pondering and rearranging the puzzle.

On my return home, things began to change. At first I was proud to see my country moving towards a more open society, changing just the little that needed to be changed, I thought. But then everything went wrong and began to fall apart. I still don't know what happened or why. I shall probably need another twenty years, if not more, to come to terms with the new situation, because I can't explain how all those wonderful people in my country turned into animals and why they decided to fight for their ideas and beliefs by killing others.

I couldn't have imagined a better place to live and bring up my children than my home town, where we lived in harmony and mutual respect. We respected each other irrespective of religion, nationality, or any other sort of distinction. That is why I am unable to explain to myself, let alone to others, all the killings and atrocities that have happened. Someone else must have done them, I sometimes think, not the people I grew up with. Did I invent all those wonderful people and the life there? No, that is impossible. I still remember everything so vividly.

I have no clear perception of my future at the moment. I think I shall go back, but I am so scared of what I might find there. What kind of people live there? They are completely different now, they lead a completely different way of life. I don't know if I will be able to like it.

V. R.
London, UK

Chapter 4: **Refugee Blues**

They Are All My Friends

I have high hopes that the war in my country will end soon. Recent peace conferences indicate there has been progress, perhaps not much, but every little bit helps. I am from a town where the population was almost equally divided: 34 per cent Serbs, 30 per cent Croats, 36 per cent minorites (Czech, Slovak, Italian and others). I had very good friends on all sides. I don't believe that war can resolve problems, which is why I am not there, fighting. I hope the war will end soon. I want people to stop killing each other. They are all my friends.

I wish Yugoslavia was what it could have been, a union, with the same rights for *one and all*, but one must be realistic. To fight for such a Yugoslavia *today* would not be very realistic. That day may come, but it may not. Right now we should stop the killing and try to achieve lasting peace, to put bread on everyone's table. The countries that emerged from the former Yugoslavia need to be rebuilt both economically and spiritually. I think it would be fair to put on trial both those responsible for the carnage and those who sacrificed the lives of innocent people for the sake of their own political goals. The 'it wasn't my fault' mentality, which resulted in such irresponsible 'leadership', needs to be eradicated. We should tell people the whole unconditional truth about what has been happening. (*Someone* must know the whole story; everyone is making such a great job of hiding it.) Then and *only* then could the issue of reuniting be raised. I know that it sounds like a dream. But that is what we should have done; not kept on killing each other.

For better or for worse, this is the age of computers. Communications will be computerized to an extent that is unimaginable today. As a future computer scientist I believe that I could do a lot to help rebuild communications in the countries of the former Yugoslavia. Communications will be the most important factor in peacetime. As a future computer scientist I cannot do much in a war, but I can do quite a lot in peacetime, which will come soon.

I am willing to go back where I come from, where all my friends are, where my parents are. I have good reasons to go back and see my people happy, and my country prosperous again.

N. M.
Lincoln, Arkansas, USA

I Was Not Willing to Take Part in This War

I left Croatia in the summer of 1991. Mobilization had begun and it was only a matter of time before I would be called up. I had done my regular military service some five years earlier, but I was not willing to join this war in any way. I decided to borrow some money and leave the country. It was a very difficult decision to make. I had been admitted to the Academy of Fine Arts in Zagreb, but I chose a life of freedom which would enable me to work and study in an environment of tolerance and understanding. I came to the Czech Republic.

An important line of distinction needs to be drawn here.

There is something which can be called 'belonging'—to a certain tradition, history, culture, or even region. One has this belonging, although one may not necessarily be aware of it, or even want it. But it does not prevent one from appreciating other cultures or traditions; understanding differences enables one to grow.

The problem begins when the basic individual feeling of belonging to a certain tradition, culture or region is manipulated (for whatever reason). That results in nationalism. When individualism is not strong enough to define itself, when it chooses to define itself on the basis of belonging to a nation (tradition, culture, history, region), that is when nationalism rears its head. What was supposed to be the foundation of growth becomes a goal one is supposed to serve.

As an artist I would simply say that I decided I could do much more for my country with a brush in my hand in exile than by pointing a gun in a nationalistic war.

I was born in Zagreb and so were my parents. But my ancestors came from Austria, Hungary, Dalmatia, and the Croatian region of Zagorje. Maybe that explains why I do not have any strong feeling of

Croatian nationalism. For me, feeling Croat is something abstract. I do not identify or perceive myself as a member of a nation, although I do know where I belong.

Actually, the place I identify with is the city of Zagreb. And one day I would like to go back there, and invest all my efforts to help the city foster a plurality of ideas, cultures and traditions. I would like to help rebuild a society able to accept, learn, develop and grow, a society without a mainstream. Zagreb is a city at the crossroads of different cultures and traditions; and it should not be the self-contained capital of a nationalistic state. I can see myself as a Croat only in the wider context of the former Yugoslavia, south-eastern Europe, and Europe as a whole.

I would like to exhibit in Zagreb one day. It already motivates my work to know that there is something else there other than war. I keep thinking about the wonderful people who are there, and who do not agree with the war. They are there, working, trying to find meaning in their work. It must be hard to live and work there if one is not in the mainstream. But it is important to know that there is more than the Zagreb which is at war, the Zagreb depicted on Croatian Television. That is motivation enough for my work, it gives me hope for the future. I only hope that one day my work will be of help to them as their work is to me now. At least as a memorial to those who refused to participate in this war.

D. I.
Prague, Czech Republic

Fear of the Draft

My main reason for leaving Sarajevo was fear of the draft. Although the situation in Yugoslavia was far from good (and was steadily deteriorating), I nearly managed to complete my studies of English language and literature at the University of Sarajevo. I made a living as a freelance translator and interpreter. (As a student I had already established myself as a reliable translator of English.) I worked for a number of companies and individuals, and was a member of the Translators' Association. For three years I translated and subtitled programmes in English for Sarajevo Television. I had more and more work and had no reason to worry about my immediate future. I intended to finish my degree and to think about postgraduate studies. But then the war broke out.

I am of fighting age, so I decided to flee.

For the last two years I have lived in Amsterdam. In June 1993 I was granted a residence permit. Since I was so close to finishing my studies in Sarajevo, I decided to inquire about the possibility of enrolling at the University of Amsterdam. On the basis of my transcripts I was told that I would only need to do the final year in order to graduate. I think this is the best and most useful thing I can do while I am here.

I plan to return to Sarajevo as soon as circumstances allow. That plan, however, depends on the risk I would run in returning. The risks are unacceptably high as long as the war continues.

I fled Yugoslavia primarily to avoid being drafted by the Yugoslav Army, the only army at the time which could legally draft me. Much has changed since then. Now there are many armies which would readily send me to the front, without asking whether I had graduated or not. Until that situation changes, I intend to stay in the Netherlands.

B. P.
Amsterdam, Holland

We All Thought It Wouldn't Be for Long

I was born in Sarajevo, and until April 1992 had spent most of my life there. When I finished high school, I enrolled in the Medical School of Sarajevo University, and passed all my mid-term exams. Then the war started and I had to leave Sarajevo. I lived with my parents near the Vrbanja Bridge, in a part of Sarajevo called Grbavica. Today it is considered Serbian territory. We are Muslims by origin, and when the Serb soldiers marched in we had to flee. We left everything behind. My parents, who did not want to leave Sarajevo, decided to stay with relatives in the centre of town. But they asked me to leave until the situation calmed down. We all thought it wouldn't be for long. So I left for Orebić, a little town on the Adriatic coast, where we had a summer house. I lived in my parents' house, I was supposed to be in my own country, but soon I discovered that I was a refugee, a refugee in what used to be my own little world. I had no money, no chance of continuing my education, and not the slightest chance of finding a job. After seven months the situation became unbearable. I could not go back to Sarajevo, and I couldn't stay in Orebić. Fortunately, I had a decent command of English, because I had spent a couple of years in an American school. So I decided to go to London and work as an au pair, until the situation in Sarajevo improved.

Unfortunately, the family I worked for were not very nice. Like many other young girls from my country, I had a very difficult time. After two months I had had enough and ran away. I applied for asylum because it was the only way for me to stay in England. I did not want to waste my time, so I took an English course, and am now trying to enrol in a university.

———

A. S.
London, UK

I Was Afraid I Would Never See My Parents Again

Home, sweet home!
When shall I be back in Prijedor?
When shall I see my friends and relatives again?
Is there any end to this fratricidal war in my country?
It is springtime now. The fields are full of flowers, birds are singing in the woods, nature is awakening. But all this beauty will not bring back the victims of the war.
I am living in Vienna now. I am trying to make a home for myself here. I have found many new friends, I have seen many famous and beautiful places, but I still yearn for my old friends, who are in exile somewhere in the West. I yearn for my home town, the river on

whose banks I spent the best times of my life, the mountain where I used to go skiing.

I receive letters from my friends, but the paper is cold, and the pen cannot trace the exact flow of their thoughts and feelings. I want to see them all. But it would take a fortune to see them. And they—with their exile visas—cannot leave the countries which have given them shelter. Among my new friends I especially like Gaga, a girl from Croatia. She is not a refugee. She came to study here in Austria. Oh, how I envy her when she goes home, 'just for the weekend', to visit her parents or friends in Zagreb.

I can still remember 5 April 1992, when the first of the thousands upon thousands of victims of the unending war in Bosnia were killed. I left Sarajevo, where I was studying, for Prijedor, my home town, still unaware that I would soon have to flee the country. Only two weeks later I was on my way to Austria. My best friends whispered in tears: 'We'll soon be together again!' My parents said the war would have to stop and promised that we would be together again soon. I am still here.

It is not easy to be so far away from one's parents, relatives and friends. And it becomes unbearable when you fear that they might be among the thousands of victims of this fratricidal war. My best friend left Prijedor in December 1992, and it was from her that I finally learned the horrible truth about the war in Bosnia and how Bosnians now live. She told me that my parents had celebrated my birthday as if I were still with them, in an attempt to forget, if only for a moment, the horror they were living. When I heard that, I was afraid I would never see my parents again. I would call them in the middle of the night, because that was the only chance to get through. I kept calling them just to make sure they were still alive. 'The whole world is waiting, but no one can help,' my dad told me the day before they decided, after sixteen months of living hell, to emigrate to Austria. They wanted to be with me and with my older brother, who was forced to leave Novi Sad only a term before he was due to graduate.

But our happiness did not last long. On 6 January 1994 my dad had a stroke and died five days later.

He will never see me teaching children.

He will never attend my graduation ceremony.

But will I ever have a graduation ceremony?

To study, one needs money, money for tuition, for room and

board, for books, for the essentials. I know many young people who had to give up their studies for want of money. They had to find jobs, which left them with no time to study.

When the war ends one day, the country will need young educated people, teachers, doctors, lawyers, architects. The Republic of Bosnia and Herzegovina is not merely a name. It is a country where we shall live together again.

I have lost fifty members of my family.

I have lost my father.

Must I lose my country as well?

A. A.

Vienna, Austria

I Spent the Best Years of My Life There

I was sixteen when I applied for a foreign exchange programme in the United States, under which I was to spend my senior year of high school in the USA, and graduate there. I was accepted by the Pacific Intercultural Exchange Program in the middle of my junior year, and was designated to live with a host family and attend a school in San Diego, California. That's how I got to the United States in September 1991.

From the moment I stepped onto American soil, all my impressions about the USA were positive. My host parents were wonderful people. I quickly made a lot of friends in school, and San Diego itself offered so many opportunities for all kinds of activities. I did not have the huge culture shock we had been warned about before leaving home. Although I was in a totally new environment, by the end of my first semester I had excellent grades, was in the top 10 per cent of my class and was placed on the principal's honours roll.

Then I started thinking about going to college in the United States. I decided to apply to several universities all over the country. I still thought that I had time to decide whether to remain in the United States (I was attracted by the idea of improving my English skills and being surrounded by people from all over the world at an American university), or go back to Bosnia (at the time, still a part of what was called Yugoslavia), and attend the University of Sarajevo, where I would be with my family and friends. What I did not know was that soon I would not be in a position to choose.

In April 1992 civil war unexpectedly broke out in Bosnia, and my native Sarajevo became the worst battlefield in the world. My mother and grandfather, with whom I used to live in Sarajevo, are now refugees in Belgrade, Yugoslavia, having lost everything they had worked for all their lives. I started to realize painfully that my much-wanted return home was becoming an increasingly distant, unreal dream. My family were no longer able to support themselves, and had started to receive humanitarian aid in Belgrade. By the end of April, I realized my return to (former) Yugoslavia had become impossible. I was no longer in a position to choose between staying in the US and going back home. Remaining in the country had become my only option. Consequently, attending college in the United States had become the only way for me to continue my college education, which I so much wanted to pursue.

By the beginning of May 1992 I had been accepted at several universities throughout the United States, one of them being the University of Florida. I discovered that UF has a very strong, competitive programme in the area of computer and information sciences, which had been my intended major for a long time. The description of the school system as a whole also attracted me, and I decided UF would academically challenge me and suit my needs best. And so in 1992 I entered the University of Florida as a freshman.

If there is one day in my life I would do anything to see happen, it is the day that I graduate from the University of Florida. I know I will be able to accomplish so much once I earn my degree. I feel very confident about my future because I believe in myself. I am a strong and capable individual who can accomplish anything if only given an opportunity to do so. I am especially confident that my field of study, computer and information sciences and mathematics, will enable me to help my native country recover once the war is over. The development of technical equipment and intelligent machines will make it possible for my native land, Bosnia-Herzegovina, and for all the countries of the former Yugoslavia which have been destroyed in this war, to catch up with the rest of the world. It will make it possible for the people to resume their normal lives. I am more than willing to take part in this process. I shall always love the country where I was born and lived most of my life, a country of which I have the most unforgettable memories.

M. S.
Gainesville, Florida, USA

The Day My Childhood Stopped

My name is A. S. and I am nineteen years old. I used to live in Sarajevo, one of the most beautiful cities in the world. This five-hundred-year-old city, rimmed by two ranges of gorgeous mountains, was my 'city of dreams', a place where people of different religions and cultures had peacefully coexisted for centuries, a place where I spent seventeen wonderful years. Today my 'city of dreams' is being destroyed in a brutal war.

The siege of Sarajevo and the war in Bosnia began on 5 April 1992. That was the day my childhood stopped and my dreams were destroyed: I witnessed the destruction of my home town. That day completely changed my life, because I was forced to leave my home, my friends, and everything I had ever had. I became a refugee in Croatia, where I lived until August 1992.

In September 1992 I went to the United States as an exchange student. I graduated from Shadow Mountain High School in Phoenix, Arizona. I wanted to continue my education in the US, so I applied to several colleges around the country. I was accepted everywhere, but only the University of Bridgeport offered me a scholarship which covered most of my expenses. Given my poor financial situation, this scholarship gave me the hope that I would be able to finish college. Still, there are additional expenses, and I am not sure I will be able to do it without someone's help.

My goal is to finish my education and to help my family, friends and country. I cannot forget the beautiful city of my childhood. I cannot forget my home. I hope that one day I will be able to go back as an educated person.

A. S.

Phoenix, Arizona, USA

This Bloody War Has Stolen Twenty Years of My Life

I left Sarajevo in April 1992 after a close friend and my uncle were badly wounded in the first week of the war. It was my mother who actually made the decision for me to leave and even then she thought she was sending me and my brother away for only a week or two. We left home with one bag each, completely unprepared for a long absence. First we went to Belgrade to stay at my uncle's. But it was much worse there than we could ever have imagined in our wildest dreams. Six of us lived in a one-bedroomed flat. We had no money. Everything was uncertain. Everyone kept saying I should enrol at Belgrade University, but I kept putting it off, hoping to return home. By May it became obvious that the situation was deteriorating. The telephone lines with Sarajevo were cut off; I realized I would miss my exams in June, and I couldn't enrol at the University of Belgrade because all the places were already filled, presumably by refugees from Croatia. Since I could not intrude on my uncle's family forever, I decided to leave Yugoslavia. The most natural place to go was the UK, because I was a student of English, and had been in England before, as an au pair.

I applied for a three-month visa, because I was absolutely positive that I would be going back home for the following academic year. But over the summer things got worse. Dozens of people I knew were killed or wounded. My parents' situation (like everyone else's) became increasingly unbearable. I finally realized that even if I did find a way to get back, my parents would not be able to support me any more. They still went to work every day, but the money they earned was next to nothing.

After settling down in England, my first priority was to go back to college. I had several reasons for wanting to continue my education, the most important being that I genuinely enjoy studying and the student way of life. I could not imagine myself doing anything else; that was the path I had chosen at home and I intended to pursue it. In England, however, that basic drive was coupled with what I can describe only as anger, a kind of bitter private protest against those who had turned my life upside down, separated me from my parents and stopped me from continuing my studies in my own home town. I wanted to show them that it is possible to rebuild one's life, to do something sensible and positive, something quite different from the madness I had witnessed. That desire grew even stronger when I realized that my parents were finally being driven out of Sarajevo, leaving behind their flat and everything they owned. It is difficult not to feel bitter when my entire family is now homeless. My parents are hopelessly wandering from one flat to another in Belgrade, relying on the hospitality of relatives and friends, with no money and slim prospects for the future. The most painful thing for me is the fact that this war has put a definite end to my life in Sarajevo. This bloody war has stolen twenty years of my life.

Thinking about the future is not only difficult, but painful, and I try to avoid it. Still, I do believe that the future lies at home. And by 'home' I mean the regions of the former Yugoslavia. I believe this not only because I know that my parents' future will depend on what I manage to do with my life, but also because I really want to return home, and make use of the knowledge I gain in England.

Even though I have always regretted leaving Sarajevo, I think that being away makes it possible to resist xenophobia and to approach the conflict with a sober head. It is too early for me to say exactly what I would like to do and where (and much of it will not depend on me anyway).

D. S.
London, UK

I Am Still in London

I was a twenty-four-year-old student of journalism who wanted to improve her English when I decided to go to England as an au pair. I was excited by the idea of leaving home for a while. I saw it as a challenge, as a chance to experience something new, an entirely different way of life, as a chance to exchange ideas with different people. Whenever I had left home before it had only been on holiday, for a few weeks, but this time I would be away for at least six months. I would have the opportunity to learn about the English way of life, and, of course, to improve my English. I never dreamed things would turn out as they did.

I left Sarajevo like someone going on a dream holiday, with all the luggage and usual things one takes when going away for more than a few weeks. My last night at home was spent with friends, telling them how excited I was about going to London. My best friend asked me to bring her a new pair of Doc Marten's from Camden Market. I shall never forget that last night with my friends in Sarajevo.

When I arrived in London, I felt like any other European. I thought how great it was to be a part of Europe, one minute in Sarajevo, the next in London. Two cities with different histories, different stories to tell. I liked the atmosphere of both airports, echoing with dozens of different languages. I thought how cosmopolitan we all were, and it made me feel a part of Europe.

The family I stayed with as an au pair was warm and the children were wonderful. I was happy with how things had turned out. But not for long. Just a few days later I saw on TV what was happening in Sarajevo. But I didn't quite understand what I saw. Strange balls of light were shooting across Sarajevo's night sky. I could not believe that these were the signs of war. When I left, only a week before, life there had been normal, people were walking in the streets, sitting in cafes, going to the shops, to school…True, war was already raging in Croatia, but it seemed far removed from us, from our town. It couldn't possibly happen to us; for God's sake, we had always lived together, we were Bosnians, not Croats, Serbs or Muslims. I was shattered. What was happening to Sarajevo, to my friends, my sister, my parents?…

I am still in London. I have been here over six months now. I don't know when I shall see my parents, my sister or my city again.

But life goes on. I am not a tourist any more. I cannot go back. My life has changed completely. After feeling anger, despair and helplessness, the time came for me to wake up.

Because of my commitment to my country and my people, I have become involved with various humanitarian organizations. It became extremely important to me to help other refugees who were often unable to speak English. I assisted them in interviews with the Housing, Health and Benefit Offices. I kept them abreast of the latest situation at home, and gave them news about other people seeking refuge in the UK.

I come from a multiethnic, multicultural society. I was brought up by my parents to respect other nations, to learn about their ways of life, and not to be afraid of differences. That has helped me to retain my sanity in the madness that has overcome Bosnia.

I would like to go home one day, but for the present that seems like just a dream. It will be a long time before I can go back to Sarajevo. Until then I shall finish my studies, and perhaps one day have the chance to help rebuild the confidence of the people of Bosnia-Herzegovina.

E. H.
London, UK

From Bosnia To America

'Bosnia, a country of beauty, brotherhood and unity…' These used to be the opening lines of almost every guidebook about my country. The war has shattered all that splendour. Happiness and laughter have been replaced by the scent of death and brute survival. I was one of many who lived in constant fear of what tomorrow might bring.

Life was becoming harder and harder. Both my parents lost their jobs. Food became a luxury. We were basically surviving on bread and salt. Life in Banja Luka, one of the Serb-conquered regions, was extremely unsafe for everybody, especially for people who did not declare themselves as Serbs. People tried to stay at home, indoors, as much as possible.

I felt trapped and depressed. The only ray of light in my life was school. It was my connection with the outside world. But then the school closed for the 'summer holidays'. Even though I was just a year away from graduating from high school, I somehow felt that for me the school doors were closed *forever*. I realized that Banja Luka would offer me no hope of continuing my education. I decided it was time for me to leave, because that was the only way to help my parents as well as myself.

In the meantime I got in touch with family friends in the United States and they generously offered to help me. But the worst was yet to come. On my way to Belgrade I faced death at every step. When I was sent back from the halfway point, I was full of fear, grief and rage, all mixed together and waiting to explode. *And they did.* That emotional energy turned into obstinacy, and it made me stronger and more persistent than ever before. I knew I *had to leave*! On 5 August I tried again to reach Belgrade, and this time I succeeded. Even though it was very hard for me to leave my parents, friends and relatives, I knew I was doing the right thing. My departure from Bosnia assured me that there was some *hope* for *all* of us.

A year and four months have passed since my first glimpse of America. I really feel I have accomplished a lot. As a graduate of West Springfield High School, with various honours and awards for academic performance, I won the top scholarship at Mount Vernon College. Being a part of this college has helped me to find myself again. Now I can fully devote myself to something I have always wanted: excellence through knowledge. And then? I already have another goal: to find a way to help my people and my country.

Although it forced me to grow up quickly, the war also broadened my perceptions. Instead of fearing what tomorrow might bring, now I clearly see myself as a part of Bosnia's future, hopefully a better one. After graduating from college I would like to return home and help my country become as beautiful as it was before the war. My experience with computers can easily be used to train others, and to improve the usage of computer information systems.

Mount Vernon College, with students from thirty-one countries and a diverse range of races, religions and backgrounds, has changed my views, broadened my mind, and made me fully aware of the diversity of people. I have learned to accept people for the good they have inside them, not for their nationality, race or religion. After the war I will have a lot more to offer those whose minds have been closed by the war.

People should realize that fighting will not make their individual lives better. No one can live *alone*, and the harmony of life is based on compromise and mutual understanding. There is no point in any kind of discrimination because every human being, no matter how different, has a lot to offer and should be appreciated for that.

I am one of many who had to leave Bosnia in order to survive. I am one of the few who had the opportunity to enter an American college. At first I felt as if I had left everybody behind; they were helpless while I selfishly went in search of a better future for myself. Now I know that whatever I accomplish can contribute to the well-being of my native country and its people. Mount Vernon College has helped me to revive that belief by teaching me that education is a crucial requirement for bringing about change.

As a strong believer in people, regardless of their religion, race or nationality, I would like to quote Robert H. Goddard: 'It is difficult to say what is impossible, for the dream of yesterday is the hope of today and reality of tomorrow.'

V. S.
Springfield, Virginia, USA

Who Knows When We'll See Sarajevo Again?

How is a young man to know if he is making the right choice? Suppose he thinks there is something special he must do with his life and afterwards finds out he wasn't suited to that at all…You could never be sure about anything for all time…You can only have the courage and strength to do what you think is right.

Irving Stone, Lust for Life

This is what I was thinking when I decided to leave my native town of Sarajevo and give myself a chance to do something more with my life than was possible in a country torn apart by nationalistic parties.

It was not an easy decision to make, and the only thing that probably gave me the courage to do it was the fact that I had already lived in another country and experienced another culture. I was fifteen when my father went to Beijing, China, representing a Yugoslav firm. The family decided to accompany him. My brother and I were accepted at the International High School in the Chinese capital, where we learned English and a bit of Chinese. Soon after the unrest at Tiananmen Square we returned to Sarajevo. I had one more year of high school to finish.

By the end of the school year I found myself in a position to choose between living a tranquil student life in a country which could not promise much because of its economic and political situation, and studying somewhere else, where I could earn a universally accepted degree. My determination to get a good education took me to France, where I was accepted at the University of Pantheon-Sorbonne in Paris, majoring in international economics. My parents stood by my decision, ready to help me.

But five months later the war erupted in Bosnia, and everything started to change. Communications were cut off, as a result of which I could no longer rely on my parents' financial and moral support. My carefree world collapsed.

I started doing a lot of small jobs, like babysitting and giving English and maths lessons. Since permission for me to stay in France depended, in a way, on my academic performance, and since I could not go back to Sarajevo, I had to get through my freshman year. And I did, in spite of the psychological turmoil I was going through.

Then came the summer. But there was no time to rest. I had to look for a more secure job and a place to live; for I could not keep imposing on the kindness of friends who had given me shelter in those difficult times. Fortunately, it took me only a couple of weeks to find a good, stable job in the Administration (*Conseil Regional d'Ile de France*). I wanted to stay sane and brave, not only for myself but for my parents as well. I had not heard from them in six months. It was not until November 1992 that they finally escaped from Sarajevo with the hope that one day they would return where they felt they belonged. But recently we found out that our house, together with everything my parents had worked for all their lives, had been looted and seized. Who knows when we'll see Sarajevo again?

My parents are now in Holland, with no job, worrying about the rest of the family trapped in Sarajevo.

Z. K.
Paris, France

We Left All Our Loved Ones Behind

I was born on 29 June 1974 in Tuzla, Bosnia, where I lived with my parents and younger sister until I was eighteen. I finished primary school in Tuzla, spent four years at music school (I played the flute), and started high school, where my main subject was languages. In high school I took part in several English language competitions. Once I came fourth in the whole of Yugoslavia. I graduated from high school in 1992.

My last year in school was very difficult for all of us.

We all felt the consequences of the war, which had already started in Croatia. We were terrified as we watched what was happening in our country. But we knew that different nationalities had been living together in Bosnia for centuries, and we did not believe that the war would spread our way. On the contrary, all my friends and I thought that 1992 was going to be a very important year in our lives because we were going to enrol at university and start a new life. Not one of us had any foreboding of war.

In 1991 I applied to several universities in England, and was accepted at Reading and Birmingham. When I received the acceptance letters it was the happiest moment of my life, for my biggest wish had come true. I am handicapped, and I worked hard throughout high school to get marks which would enable me to study in England and earn a good degree. I decided to study in England because I had had hospital treatment there, and it was where my doctor, who had treated me since I was three, lived.

But on 15 May 1992 all my dreams were shattered: my home town was attacked, and for the first time in my life I heard shells and bombs explode. I saw soldiers in the streets, heard sirens and witnessed destruction. I felt afraid and helpless. I spent four months liv-

96

ing in agony and fear, mainly hiding in the cellar with my parents and sister. On 20 September 1992 my parents decided that it was time to leave because I was having health problems, and was running out of life-sustaining medicine which it was impossible to buy or get. So we left in a small car, taking only the bare essentials. We left all our loved ones behind, our family and friends. That was the hardest thing of all.

When we arrived in England, we registered as refugees, and I tried to continue my education. Although I had places at two universities, financial problems made it impossible for me to enrol. So as not to lose a year, I attended Park Lane College in Leeds, where I did a German 'A'-level and RSA III in English. In June 1993 I passed my exams with top marks.

While I was at Park Lane College I applied again to several universities, and received unconditional offers from the universities of York, Durham, and Essex. I started at York University as a full-time student in October 1993. I received a grant from the Local Education Authority in Leeds. It helps to cover my living expenses, but it is not enough to cover everything, because, given my serious health problems and difficulties in walking, I need a lot of extra things, such as vitamins and walking aids. I have therefore decided to apply for the Open Society Institute's grant, which would make my situation much easier and help me to finish my studies. I hope to return to my country, health permitting. I would like to help young people there get a better education, and a better chance for the future they hope for.

V. K.
York, UK

My Heart Is Elsewhere

I was born and raised in Banja Luka (population: 150,000), a small provincial town in northern Bosnia. I attended school there and enrolled in the Electrical Engineering Department of Banja Luka University. In 1992 I was only six exams away from my degree when hell broke loose.

The year before we had heard echoes of the fighting in Croatia. Soon all the boys were being sent to the front. The university became a gloomy place. Still, it all seemed to be happening on another planet. The body bags were the first ominous sign. The fighting was elsewhere, but the dead and wounded entered our reality.

Then it flared up in Sarajevo, and suddenly we had a curfew, shops were looted, and all semblance of 'normal' life disappeared. Classes at the university were held irregularly; there was no heating. We slept as in medieval times, going to bed at sunset, because there was no electricity. The black market, with its colourful trappings, was another world.

There were other disturbing things as well. First of all, there was the shooting. Day and night, from the mountains, but also from the outskirts of town. Armed men started appearing in the city. People began to disappear. Many were attacked in the street. You only felt safe at home. But then even to stay at home became risky. Various army groups and police units could burst in looking for new recruits or just for a bit of fun.

Life became unbearable, unworthy of human beings. I had to leave. Family friends in Holland offered to help and I left home in an ambulance, pretending to be sick, and in need of special treatment. Of course, I paid 500 Deutschmarks for certain people to look the other way.

In Holland my host family and the authorities provided all possible help. I enrolled in the Government Programme for Refugees from the Former Yugoslavia. In due course I was granted 'A' status, meaning that I became a refugee as defined in international treaties. At the same time I was given the right to stay in the Netherlands, to work or study.

It seems pointless to explain that here I am in a position to keep abreast with specialized reading. The library in Banja Luka was never very rich, but now I am not sure that it even exists any more. Laboratories were equipped only with the essentials. I got used to that. Here I am learning how to use new equipment. The opportunity to study at Delft University is a real eye-opener, and it allows me to keep up with my chosen profession.

But what next? Frankly, I don't know. For the time being I certainly intend to finish my studies here. I feel that the knowledge I am obtaining here would be useful anywhere. Still, this is not my country. I speak the language, I have Dutch friends, but I am still a stranger. And my heart is elsewhere. On the other hand, I don't want my country to remain as it is now. I know that we Bosnians are the only ones who can do something there. Therefore I shall go back. I feel it in my bones. I know that my technical skills and knowledge will be of use in that war-devastated country. What I am not sure about is how I would adapt to the mental state of that society, which made me leave the country in the first place. That has to change.

D. M.
Amsterdam, Holland

I Wanted More Than That

It was on 15 May 1992 that the war began in my home town, Tuzla. A brutal end was put to normal life, or—more to the point—it completely changed, because life under brutal wartime conditions became normal.

For me, time passed slowly, in constant anticipation of more shelling, but also in the hope that I would not be among the many wounded or killed. Most days we spent in the cellar, in fear that the enemy might storm our part of the city, and start looting, raping and killing. That fear was the worst of all.

I read a lot, but by the end of the summer I had read everything I could find. I had attended too many funerals, and used up all the tranquillizers we had in the house. Soon I started to think about leaving town, my parents, my family. Not running away, but doing something for myself, and for them as well. So I joined a convoy which was going to Zagreb, Croatia. From Zagreb I got in touch with my friends in England in the hope that I would find a family to stay with.

I arrived in London on 22 September 1992.

For the first month I worked as an au pair, looking after a baby. At the time I was not thinking about seeking asylum, because I thought that as long as I stayed with that family I would be safe and protected. But it did not work out. I had to change jobs. I found a new family and stayed with them for nine months. She was an Indian lady who was suffering from cancer, and had two children. Her husband had left her. I was the cleaner, cook and a sort of 'stepmother', because I had to look after her, the children and the house. The only thing I managed to do was finish an English course. But I knew that I wanted more than that.

Encouraged by some friends, I decided to seek asylum. I found a small flat and started a new life. As a part-time student, it will take another year for me to complete the course I have been doing at Kingston University. They recognized all the exams I had passed at Sarajevo University, and accepted me in the final year. So everything looks perfect. Except that sometimes I wish I were nearer my family. I am not nostalgic by nature, but worry makes me homesick.

As for my future plans, all I can say is: 'I don't know!' Being ambitious and still quite young, I would like to be a member of a pro-gressive-thinking community. If I have the chance to stay here, I would like to do so. But if they need me in Tuzla, in Bosnia, I will go. After all, that is where my home is, that is where I come from. For now I would like to study, because knowledge is the only passport which is valid everywhere.

(Perhaps this essay should be longer, but my soul is empty and wounded, and I want to forget all the things that happened to me.)

A. O.
London, UK

It Is Very Difficult to Find a Place for Us

When the war started in Bosnia-Herzegovina, I was in a very difficult situation. My mother had been in hospital because of psy-chological problems brought on by my father's death from cancer sev-eral months before. The growing atmosphere of violence and fear only worsened her condition. We lived alone. Soon after the war started we ran out of food. We were helpless, because there was no water in our neighbourhood, no electricity in town. We barely managed to get bread. We were frightened, and felt vulnerable and alone.

During all those months the University of Sarajevo remained open, and I attended classes as often as I could. I was studying musicology and it was my last year. I kept on studying, because it helped me to keep my sanity in those miserable times. Like other students, and my friends, I did not want to let the war destroy my future. With the help of our professors we music students tried to fight the ills of war and to live as normally as possible.

But in November, after eight months of war, I decided to leave; I was afraid that my mother might fall ill again, because of the constant stress and poor nutrition (she weighed only eighty pounds at the time). My mother did not want to go; her whole life was there, in that town. But I knew that she would not survive the winter. We were both very weak, and exhausted. My tutor was also about to leave town, and I felt that my only possible line of escape—my studies—was vanishing too.

We left Sarajevo on 25 November 1992 with a Red Cross convoy for sick women and children. I shall never forget that sad day. We were so scared and unhappy, because we were leaving everything behind, our home, our friends, our lives. And we did not know when, if ever, we would be able to come back. I have a very small family, but now we are split up all over the world—in the former Yugoslavia, in England, in Israel. It is terrible. I know I am lucky to have escaped the worst misfortunes of war, but I don't think I was lucky to have been pushed out and expelled from my home and my homeland.

After four months in Belgrade, where we stayed with several different host families, we arrived in Spain on 10 April 1993, once again with the same feeling of fear, uncertainty and vulnerability. A Spanish friend of ours had sent us air tickets and a letter of invitation. But that excluded us from the Spanish Refugees Programme. We spent seven months in a little village, with some other people, waiting to be finally registered as refugees. In October we were allowed to go to Madrid, where we now live with a host family, but still on a temporary basis. (It's very difficult to find a place for us.) I work in the family restaurant, five hours a day, without wages and without any state support. In fact, we are now waiting for residence permits. But it's all taking a long time, and meanwhile I am not allowed to work officially.

Next year, if I am lucky, I shall graduate from the Musicology Department of the Complutenel University of Madrid. Fortunately, the Ferraz Conservatory made a great exception and waived my tuition fees. I really appreciate it. The Academy of Music in Sarajevo is held in very high regard, and I was just about to graduate when the war broke out. That is why I am rather successful now.

I know that it is a privilege to be able to study, as a refugee, in these humiliating circumstances. I am determined to finish my studies as soon as possible. It will be very hard, but I am sure I can do it. I work hard, and I am doing quite well. But I really need some help. With a grant I could rent a small apartment, and still work part-time in the restaurant for some extra money. Then I would manage to live and study. Now I have only 300 dollars from a donation, which I spend only on the bare essentials. And I don't know what I shall do when it runs out.

My duty now is to survive, but also to prepare myself for after the war. My greatest wish is to go back home. Sometimes I think the war is never going to end. And I know what life there looks like. My friends there live in deplorable conditions. Once a month I manage to get in touch with some of them via ham radio. I know how desperate and hopeless they feel. Sometimes I wish I'd never left them, I wish I'd shared the fate of my town. And then I begin to think about what I can do for them when I go back.

I don't hate any of them, any of the nationalities of the former Yugoslavia. We are all victims. My late father was Orthodox, from Montenegro, my mother is a Catholic Croat. And they loved each other. Now we shall have to fight against this hate which has risen among us. And after the war we shall have to learn how to live together again. I could work for that, perhaps as a teacher, perhaps as a musician, revealing the richness of diversity through music.

I want to go back home, but I want to live in peace, with respect for human rights, under the rule of law. This will be a difficult task, and it will require painful, long-term efforts on the part of us all. And I really want to be involved in that, and to help in any possible way. I can't bear all the destruction, all the misery of my people, of my country. I still can't believe all this has really happened. And I don't want to be a refugee all my life. I ought to go home and live with my people. *Please, help me.*

N. Z.
Madrid, Spain

I Still Have Many Years Ahead

The present situation in my country makes it clear why I was forced to leave Bosnia. I was fortunate to escape the horrors of war, which has not been the case with many young people my age. I arrived in the UK hoping that the war would soon be over, and that I would quickly return home to join my family and begin to study. Now my family is scattered all over the world. I stayed in London, still hoping that all the destruction which so affected my life was only a nightmare.

I come from Doboj, a small provincial town in north-east Bosnia, where I spent a happy, contented childhood. I finished high school there, and six years of piano. But the war changed everything. I left Bosnia a few days after it broke out. I spent the first six months in Croatia, but I was miserable because my parents were trapped in the occupied city, without knowing where my sister and I were. After many sleepless nights, I received great news: my parents had managed to get out of the war zone. After a brief family reunion, my mother left for Germany, my father joined the army, and I decided to return to England.

I am only twenty, and I still have many years ahead. In order to make the best of my life I have to study and improve my knowledge. Since my parents are unable to support me financially, I now depend on the moral and financial support of others.

M. S.
London, UK

I Am Twenty-One

My name is H.M. I am twenty-one. I come from Bosnia-Herzegovina. I was born in Mostar. In 1992, when the war started, I had just finished high school and, full of the optimism of youth, enrolled at the Law School of the University of Mostar. At the time nobody believed all the rumours about war coming to Bosnia. Nobody could see any reason for it; most people minded their own business, convinced that the ills of the present would soon pass. I looked to the future with optimism. (Even now I am an optimist, and I hope for a solution to the catastrophic situation in my homeland.)

It was not easy without food, water, electricity and other essentials. But I did not give up hope. Despite the daily shelling, and all the other ills of war, I continued to study. I remember how I would go over all my maths, English and German lessons from high school, because they were the only books I had in the cellar where I lived with my parents, brother and neighbours. It was terrifying to see how many people went missing and disappeared without a word. But I did not lose hope, and the more people talked about the horrors of war, the more determined I was to study. This, I thought, is my only escape.

In my opinion, the only way to put an end to the atrocities of war is to bring new people into power. My country needs intelligent, young, educated and, above all, ambitious, energetic and optimistic people, capable of making radical changes. The ordinary people simply followed their leaders like a flock of sheep. But who were their leaders? Did they ever ask themselves that? How could they believe that genocide would give anyone a better future? Poor people, how fooled they were. I get so angry when I think about the politicians in my country. They destroyed everything we had. Everything except hope.

I refuse to reject my friends because of their nationality or religion. We are all equal. We still write to each other, despite the distance that separates us. The advocates of war should see these letters, which are full of love, nostalgia for the time we spent together, and hope that we shall see each other again. We have to give our best to help renew Bosnia-Herzegovina. The future needs a special kind of people, people with motivation, a sense of responsibility and self-confidence. First of all, of course, we need democracy, freedom, tolerance. We must not make a difference between people just because of their nationality or religion. Everyone has the right to live; we are all human beings. That is why I don't understand the leaders waging this bloody war. Are they human? I often wonder whether they feel at least some guilt for the deaths of so many innocent people? There are so many questions I can't answer. But I know that there is one way to find the answer, and that is to stop the war and let my people have a better future. I want to be a part of it.

H. M.
London, UK

France Is Great, But France Isn't Home

I was born on 22 March 1975 in Sarajevo. I left my home town on 24 April 1992. I was forced to leave by the shells and bullets. My parents stayed behind.

I did not speak a word of French when I arrived in France. During the summer of 1992 I took an intensive French course at the Alliance Française. I was subsequently accepted at the Lycée Saint-Thomas d'Aquin for the 1992–93 school year in the class of *première S (Scientifique)*, where the emphasis is on the sciences. That suited me well, because in Sarajevo I had gone to a high school which was renowned for its extensive programme in mathematics, physics, and computer sciences, and I had been an excellent student. This year I am preparing for the exams which will allow me to study electrical engineering at university.

These past two years have been very difficult for me. I have been hoping and praying for peace in Bosnia, telling myself that this madness cannot go on much longer. I wanted to go back. My parents were there. My friends were there. My home is there. France is great, but France isn't home. My dilemma was terrible, but it was resolved in a way that was even more terrible. My father was badly wounded by a sniper on 18 January 1994, and brought to France for medical treatment. My mother accompanied him, since his condition required constant care. The doctor said that my father would need at least two years of treatment and several operations. Now I have to stay in France to help him.

S. R.
Paris, France

My Aim Is to Follow My Path

Ever since childhood my two main interests have been writing and the cinema.

In 1990, after finishing high school, I was accepted at the University of Sarajevo to study journalism. But I decided to spend a year in London first and improve my English, because a good command of English would help me in my future career. So I went to England for a year, mastered the language, and just when I was thinking of returning to Yugoslavia the war broke out. I was forced to stay in England, and reconsider my plans.

I quickly realized that journalism was a fiercely competitive profession in England, requiring a very high standard of English, which I had yet to attain. So I reorientated myself towards studying film, my other main field of interest. I had had a film laboratory in Sarajevo, and had read quite a lot of books about my favourite films and directors. So I decided to take 'A'-level film and communication studies at South Thames College, and on the strength of my grades I was accepted at the University of North London. During my 'A'-level course I joined a team of students making short films.

The more I work on film (practice and theory), the more convinced I am (especially considering the feedback I get from my studies and tutors) that this is an area in which I can do something worthwhile for myself, and thus for my country as well.

I derive a lot of satisfaction from both my studies and my practical work, and this motivates me to learn more. I find myself delving into various aspects of film, exploring all angles of film technique and scriptwriting.

I see myself working in the film industry, my aspiration being to become a director. I am learning to appreciate the strengths and weaknesses of American, European, Asian and Third World cinema. I believe that in order to create something worthwhile, one must be aware of history, of current and future trends, of commercialism and avant-gardism, and find one's own place. An artist must have a global outlook, knowledge and appreciation of cultures, yet formulate and retain his/her own style. I feel European; this comes from my roots and my culture.

I would like to complete my studies abroad, to work and make my own films, and then to return to my native land and help develop the film industry there.

My aim is to follow my path of accomplishment in Europe and/or the US, while keeping a watchful eye on developments in my native Bosnia and Sarajevo.

I hope we are now seeing the beginning of the end of the war in Bosnia. Bosnia will have to be rebuilt, and it may take years before the film industry develops there again. There used to be such a rich artistic life in Sarajevo, particularly because of the city's multiethnic cultural identity. I will have to see how the new Bosnia shapes up and what role I can have in the new environment.

Bosnians as I knew them always felt an urge to project the beauty and mystery of their country through the arts. I see myself as one of them, and this is my long-term dream and aim.

N. P.
London, UK

Part II

Stories of Disillusionment, Despair and Hope

'In my heart I am still tied to the people of a country that officially doesn't exist any more.'

Chapter 5: **Reflections**

War in Yugoslavia—War Within Myself

Two years ago the crumbling communist regime in my country was trying to tighten the belt of the Yugoslav people for the last time. My parents, who both hold doctorates, were having a hard time providing food and basic clothing for the family. Everyone had lost the grandiose ideals of working for the 'common good'. The forty-year-old machinery of the 'dictatorship of the proletariat' was facing defeat.

At the same time, throughout the country, there was growing appreciation of historical tradition. In Serbia, everyone was celebrating long-forgotten holidays, waving the old Serbian flags; publications and shop-windows returned to the old Cyrillic alphabet; there was a sense of rebirth in the air. A culture that had been 'stifled for centuries' was revived in a matter of weeks. Serbia was not alone in its renaissance—people all over Yugoslavia became much more aware of their origins, customs and religion. The richness of tradition and cultural diversity could be felt everywhere.

People suddenly felt reunited, much as they did during the post Second World War euphoria, except for one thing: the sense of togetherness did not extend beyond the boundaries of one's own particular nationality or religion. Overnight Serbo-Croatian, the predominantly spoken language, became two separate languages: Serbian and Croatian. What initially seemed to be cultural appreciation and patriotism developed into a complete misunderstanding and depreciation of other cultures and then into various separatist movements. The treacheries and massacres of the Second World War, so carefully put aside by the communists, were laid bare again, for no other reason than to show how the quisling forces of each Yugoslav nation had harmed the others.

At the time I saw the situation with the same eyes as everyone around me. I simply became one of millions of Serb nationalist voices in Yugoslavia. I remembered that I had never known my grandfather—

he had been hanged by the Ustashas (Croatian quislings). I remembered being told that my family had not been allowed to take him off the gallows for four days because the Ustashas were setting an example for the rest of the village. And I resented the Croats for that.

But at the same time I knew that there was nothing intrinsically evil about the Croats, and nothing inherently altruistic about the Serbs. The Croats' reasons for hating the Serbs seemed reasonable, too. Furthermore, some of my best friends were Croats. I could not resolve the dilemma between love for my own culture and respect for cultures that differed from mine. Long before the war erupted in my homeland, there was a war going on inside my head—a war in which I was fighting myself.

The only way to stop the war in my mind was to gain perspective. Fortunately, I was accepted at East Carolina University in the United States. After completing my fourth year of high school, I crossed the Atlantic as a seventeen-year-old with a suitcase in each hand and the desire to find answers to the questions burning within me. Living in the States for a year, I encountered entirely different cultures and outlooks. I learned that there was no single correct view of the world, no one outlook that was somehow better than others. I began to understand the subjective nature of thoughts and opinions. I saw people dealing with problems that were very different from those in my country. I started seeing the 'larger picture', a picture where no nation is sufficient unto itself, a picture where each culture, however unique and special it may seem, is just a part of the bigger cultural mosaic of the world. This realization has helped me to resolve my own private war.

Now I know that all my justification and rationalization of the Serbian nationalist movement was irrelevant, because each claim inevitably started from a set of prejudices and beliefs that placed one people above another. Now I see that the conflict in Yugoslavia is really due to an inability to forget the past—a past that was at times certainly bloody, fraudulent and malignant. During the forty years of the 'dictatorship of the proletariat' in Yugoslavia, 'forgetting' the past was an act imposed by the rulers, not an act of the heart. The recent demise of communism in Yugoslavia released the demons of nationalism, and the inability to forgive the injustices of the past. Someone had to be blamed for the hardships of everyday life, and nothing is easier than to blame others for one's own misfortunes. The seamless mesh of these two factors, strengthened and perpetuated by gruesome media abuse, culminated in civil war. Once this was 'achieved', even the most open-minded people took sides, blaming others for the pain of their wartime losses.

While I seem to have stopped the war inside my head, my country is still being torn apart by a senseless violence. The unspoken pain of a homeland entangled in a civil war is constantly with me. My own understanding of the issues has not helped to resolve the conflict. This is why I am eager to return home. I believe that my experience, like that of any other Yugoslav abroad, can bring understanding among the people of my country. I hope that my Bosnian, Croat and Serb brothers will soon see the futility of hatred, and realize that avenging the past will do no one any good.

J. P.
Corvallis, Oregon, USA

We Refused to Take Sides

My husband and I left Yugoslavia for Czechoslovakia in August 1991, hoping that the turmoil in our country would be only temporary. My husband had been drafted as a reservist with the Yugoslav People's Army to fight in Croatia. At the time I had successfully completed my first degree at the University of Belgrade and was working for B-92, the Belgrade radio station. I was reluctant to give up my work with such an effective and useful voice of moderation. We considered ourselves Yugoslavs (and still do) and refused to take sides in a conflict to which we had the deepest political and conscientious objections. But the situation deteriorated and we were forced to reconcile ourselves to prolonged exile. As educated young people we had to consider how we could contribute to the processes of reconciliation.

Since we wanted to continue our education, we were very happy to accept an invitation for my husband to take up a training fellowship at the University of Kent in Canterbury, UK. I started work on my MA degree in June 1993, studying the culture of totalitarian states. In August 1992 I took part in a conference on the conflict in the former Yugoslavia, organized by the Department of Communication and Image Studies at the University of Kent, Canterbury. In researching my MA I stayed in touch with the department, and when I completed my degree I received an offer from the University of Kent to do a PhD degree on the topic of 'Hate Images' and the part played by visual propaganda in fuelling the conflict in my country. Since leaving the former Yugoslavia I have maintained regular contact with Radio B-92, and have continued to work as their correspondent and representative in Britain. I have sought to promote the activities of Radio B-92 and other independent media in the former Yugoslavia. In October 1993, for instance, I addressed a conference in Sheffield organized by supporters of community radio. I believe that these activities and this experience will give me some of the necessary skills to help rebuild a civil society in my native country. I am convinced that those forced to leave Yugoslavia must be prepared to return, so that their exile can be put to good use. It is certainly my intention to return home and resume my work in academia and with the independent media, defending the battered principles of tolerance, pluralism and democracy, in which I believe passionately.

S. P.
Canterbury, UK

Only Because I Was Not One of Them

War is horrid.
Not everyone can understand it.
Not everyone wants to support it.
Not everyone can.

Yugoslavia was falling apart. What was once my homeland had become a scene of horror and despair. Grotesque images on television, senseless destruction, thousands of deaths. Why?

People were fighting wars in their heads, on the ground, in the air, in their homes. It was impossible not to get involved. Asking questions became pointless and stating one's opinion in public became risky. At seventeen no one sits idly by and watches. It is my generation that will have to carry on living in this land, suffering its mistakes.

To disagree with the prevailing political credo and the government was dangerous. As time passed, I became aware of things that had not been important to me before. My mother is Muslim, my father Croatian, but he was born in Belgrade and brought up a Yugoslav. The time came when I had to decide what to be: Muslim? Serb? Croat? Or simply disappear. Phone calls in the middle of the night, strange looks, living in fear that someone would knock on my door with a gun in his hand. And why? Merely because I was not one of *them*. For anyone who once knew Belgrade, that was something unimaginable.

The political power struggle in Belgrade turned out to be even more ruthless than the one in Bosnia. National hatred flooded the streets, turning neighbour against neighbour. My whole world was falling apart. Some of my family from Bosnia managed to move to Serbia. Some of them never called. Life was getting worse and gradually I stopped feeling at home. One by one my friends were leaving the country in search of a better place to study and live, either temporarily or for good. I decided to leave too, to forget as much as possible, to find a place where I could dedicate my time to learning and studying. England was the country I loved. Even before I ever visited it, I had mental images of Hyde Park, Oxford Street, Buckingham Palace… Mesmerized by the beauty of the English language I would spend hours in the British Council in Belgrade, watching British films, reading the plays and poetry of Oscar Wilde, Shakespeare, Blake and others. I derived great pleasure from reading a book in the original and translating newspaper articles for my father. In the afternoons I attended language classes at various language institutes and dreamed of going to England and drinking in its culture and traditions.

I was twelve when I first set foot on English soil. I visited it often after that, but always with the feeling of being away from home. Memories of times spent in Brighton, Oxford and London, of long-lasting friendships and a different way of life, meant a lot to me. And when the war started, the English way of life seemed much closer to me than the 'new' wartime life of Belgrade.

A friend who was studying in England sent me the relevant information about British universities and I applied. The schooling system suited my pace and expectations. A British university degree is recognized all over the world, and English is the language I love and can speak best. Soon an offer from one of the universities arrived and the choice was made. I left Belgrade, which was no longer mine.

What now?

When your past is shattered, your future becomes clear. During my last year of high school everything was blurred, and I felt lost. I no longer had a clear idea of my future. The unemployment rate in Yugoslavia was soaring, and there were no jobs in my own area of interest.

In a country at war, only politicians and soldiers can find work. Mathematicians and computer programmers do not fit into the political bureaucracy. Most scientists and engineers found that they were no longer in a position to do the job they had been trained for. In order to survive, people were forced to smuggle cigarettes and food and sell them on the black market. Until the time comes when mathematicians do maths and programmers write applications and programmes I have no future in Yugoslavia.

Since 1991 the Yugoslav market has been gradually shutting down. Industry was the worst affected by the pressures of war. Almost all big foreign companies withdrew from the market, and the computer industry was no exception.

The biggest scar left on the face of Yugoslavia will be the lack of university-educated people. Industry and the economy have fallen far behind the rest of Europe, and will have to be rebuilt. Someone must acquire the knowledge to contribute to this process.

One can hardly expect foreign postwar investment in the current market's obsolete technology. I see myself as helping to introduce new technologies. Modern industrial strategy will have to be tailored to EU standards. A shortage of machinery is somehow easier to cope with than lack of experience.

Now I can devote myself to science. One day I hope my country will be able to benefit from what I am learning here. Having time to concentrate on the right things is very important. I cannot fight a war or be a politician. I wasn't born for it. My idea is to study, to specialize in the one field that has always been my main interest. Then I will be ready to fight any war against poor education; to help those who need to learn, and to train them to pass their knowledge on to younger generations; to show people how a developed country fights ignorance. That would be the greatest victory.

A. B.
London, UK

If We Cannot Be in the Same Country, the Least We Can Do Is Create a Peaceful Neighbourhood

My name is V.D. and I am from Belgrade, Yugoslavia. I arrived in the USA in October 1992. I applied to several universities, and after receiving a full tuition scholarship from DePauw University in Greencastle, Indiana, I decided to stay and continue my education there. DePauw is a small, excellent liberal arts college, which offers a very strong undergraduate programme. It is a very open-minded and dynamic place, where students are directly involved in all spheres of university life.

Why did I leave Yugoslavia? Having refused to go and fight in the war, and having been involved in the anti-war student demonstrations of 1992 in Belgrade, I was concerned for my personal safety. I had tried, together with my friends, to oppose the war policy of the current communist regime, but guns turned out to be much more powerful weapons than the spoken word. That was perhaps the last attempt to stop the tragedy which has torn the territory of the former Yugoslavia apart.

I have just completed my first semester at DePauw University as a philosophy and economics major. My education is of great importance to me because that is the only way I can help my suffering country. Getting a western education is especially important because it will make me ready, when the time comes, to help rebuild my country. I think I have chosen my majors well. Philosophy will help me to understand why my people see their history and existence the way they do. Economics will enable me to help build a new society, based on the free market, equal opportunities and justice for all. That kind of knowledge will put me in tune with the principles of democracy, which will help me contribute to creating an open and free society in my country.

I would really like to be involved in my country's future intellectual and political life, to ensure a brighter future for coming generations, and fair relations among the countries of the former Yugoslavia. If we cannot be in the same country, the least we can do is create a peaceful neighbourhood. I would like to see these countries reestablish their broken ties, economic relations and political tolerance.

My country has had economic sanctions imposed on it because of its blind, anti-democratic regime and that regime's violent policy towards Bosnia. I had hoped the bloodshed would stop, and this would help to build new relations. But a better way is to assist the education of young people from these countries.

The Supplementary Grant Program for Students from the Former Yugoslavia is a wonderful idea which will make change possible. We have to establish freedom of speech, a new legal system and a new economy. Students from the former Yugoslavia could make these changes and correct their parents' mistakes. By investing in the education of young people you are investing in the future, in peace and in prosperity. Our experience and knowledge will, I hope, help to open the minds as well as the borders of our countries.

V. D.
Greencastle, Indiana, USA

We Have to Communicate

There were several reasons why I left Yugoslavia. Compared to the majority of young people who left the country because of the war, I must admit that I was not directly affected by its economic, political or existential consequences. I had a job, I was able to support myself, I was not discriminated against, my life and my possessions were not in danger. But I was unable to communicate with my family and friends in the war areas. Like many other people experiencing a sense of loss, I lived under constant stress because of the lack of communication.

Living without information, letters, phone calls, contact, made me aware of how my personal situation reflected the symptoms of an isolated society.

My professional duties, counselling emotionally disturbed families, kept reminding me of the importance of communication and dialogue in resolving mental problems. It was so obvious that this model could be applied in efforts to resolve the social crisis, but unfortunately it was abandoned. Having experience in the use of drama as a means of education, I had the opportunity to explore the enormous possibilities of gaining new insight through the arts. Although not an artist myself, it helped me to understand how art communicates meaning. Studying the arts and culture, I am now more interested in interpreting human intersubjective reality as expressed through language. As creators of their intersubjective reality, artists can communicate it to their audience, and this process is especially important in education. After finishing my course at the university, I would like to explore how changes of meaning occur in the process of dialogue between author and audience, particularly between artist and children. This is a field I would like to pursue when I go back home and join other experts in Belgrade, working on various projects in art education.

My personal plans and hopes after completing the course are to reunite members of my family living in Croatia and Bosnia. I have had no news of some of them for more than a year. But instead of succumbing to despair, I have been getting in touch with other separated families who were unknown to me before. I feel that through communication we can bridge our differences, and that one day we shall be able to feel at home wherever we live, as long as we know each other, and make more room for real dialogue. Bosnia will be a good starting place to talk about open society. Naturally, the idea of the open society cannot feed, heal or bring peace. But, like a utopia or a fairy tale, it can initiate new meanings about a better life. After a war like this one, nothing can be more important.

Lj. K.
Warwick, UK

What Comes After This Bad Dream?

'Don't touch my figures,' Archimedes reportedly said to the Roman soldiers conquering his country. Unimpressed by his words or his figures, they killed him.

Archimedes was trying to ignore the brutal world he lived in. He kept working on his geometry while killing and destruction were going on all around him, and he ended up getting killed himself. It may appear lofty and dignified to do what one considers to be important in life regardless of the external circumstances, but sometimes it just doesn't work. If one wants to remain true to what one considers ultimately important or worthwhile (to philosophy, for instance, or the arts, science, or indeed geometry), one must have the minimum conditions for pursuing such activities.

By 1991 most of the young people in Belgrade (where I spent most of my life prior to leaving for the USA), probably like their counterparts in other parts of the former Yugoslavia, were not living, behaving or thinking as they used to. Things that were once important to them, ceased to have any significance at all. The 'usual' problems of the young gave way to much more serious problems, which threatened their future. The source of these problems, of course, lay in the domain of politics, primarily in the war that was beginning 'elsewhere', but was still nearby, in what used to be our country. Football and basketball games, school work and related problems, new and old acquaintances, girlfriends and boyfriends, partying, even the ever-present problem common to 99 per cent of all college students—being permanently broke—were no longer our primary topics of conversation or thought. It became virtually impossible for young college students (at least among the people I knew) to talk for more than fifteen minutes without touching upon politics, and in particular the war. We in Belgrade lived relatively far away from where the real war and killing were going on; however, slowly but surely it was becoming a part of our own reality, and the main source of our fears and frustrations. In early 1991, a few of us were still trying to delude ourselves that the deep Yugoslav crisis and all its antagonisms could be resolved without violence or bloodshed. But after the first bullets were fired in Serb-populated and mixed regions of Croatia, it became more and more apparent that the country was heading towards war, not peace. The armed conflict in Slovenia was, relatively speaking, too brief and, compared with what followed, too 'painless' for most of the people where I lived to take seriously; but the war in Croatia, and especially the Vukovar campaign, became a major source of fear and frustration in Belgrade (the biggest reason probably being that quite a number of people from Belgrade—including several of my own friends—were drafted for the Vukovar campaign). After the battle for Vukovar, tensions calmed down a little, and the arrival of UNPROFOR in some of the disputed regions in Croatia (Krajina) gave some reason to hope that the ethnic war in the former Yugoslavia might come to an end. Unfortunately, that was just another illusion, and in the spring of 1992 the first bullets were fired in Bosnia; by early summer there was full-scale war, taking the largest toll of all the armed conflicts that have ravaged the former Yugoslavia in the last three and a half years. Its end, I am afraid, is not in sight.

Someone may have good reason to ask: What is the connection between what I have just described and the legend about Archimedes? Well, without wishing to make any inappropriate comparisons, I would like to say that we all probably have our own figures. I love science. I love mathematics, physics and astronomy, and I hope to make a lasting contribution to these fields one day. I wasn't a top student of engineering, but I was a very promising student of astronomy, and, most importantly, I loved it, I enjoyed studying. But like all other aspects of normal life, it was spoiled by what was happening around me.

Even before the war started, Yugoslavia was suffering badly from the 'brain drain', i.e. the most educated individuals and professionals were seeking ways to leave the country (usually shortly after obtaining their university or postgraduate degree), and many of them left for good. Since 1991, the already heavy toll being paid by most of the former Yugoslavia in one of their most valuable (but least appreciated) 'hard currencies'—educated professionals—has started increasing. But an important distinction must be made between those who are planning to return, and those who are not. I see myself in the former category, in spite of everything. I want to go back one day— and not as a foreign tourist, or what we used to call back home a *gastarbeiter* (from the German, meaning Yugoslavs temporarily working abroad). I want to go back for good, and to help rebuild my country and its society.

Needless to say, I hope that peace will reign over the whole region by then, that the destruction will be over, and that the rebuilding of all parts of Yugoslavia, and their cultural, political, spiritual, economic and democratic renaissance, will be on its way. In the short term, I am not a great optimist, but in the long run I believe in a very different Balkans from the one we have now. My generation is still young enough to expect renewal and renaissance, in a Serbia different from what it is now—with my generation (and those younger than us) making it a different, better place to live. That's why I plan to go back; hopefully, the storm of war will be over, but real reconstruction and renewal can start only when this nightmare comes to an end. I don't think I am escaping from the hard work of rebuilding, I am just escaping from the present madness.

When the time comes for the toughest and most challenging, responsible work of rebuilding what has been destroyed and reconstructing from the ruins that are left—I expect to be there. I feel my participation in that renewal as both a great challenge and a moral duty.

That is why I plan to be there for the new dawning which, I am convinced, will have to follow this bad dream.

A. B.
USA

It Was Not Easy to Decide

'Leaving home is never easy, even when such a decision is considered in "normal" circumstances. God knows how tough it is to leave everything behind without knowing whether one will ever be able to go back.'

These were the words of Victor Souza, a Portuguese businessman, who had to emigrate from Portugal when he was sixteen. I met him just a month after my arrival in Portugal. Mr Souza's words hit home, because that was just how I felt at the time, consumed with self-pity. His words stayed with me as I began to think about my future in Portugal.

The arrival of 'democracy' and 'national liberty' in the former Yugoslavia gave rise to hatred, and to war. This deprived a lot of young people of any chance to start a career. Frustrated by the apparent impossibility of any political change (with the war escalating and the opposition divided), I began to think of leaving the country. As Mr Souza said: 'It was not easy to decide.' My father died six months before I left, and, being the eldest son in the family, I became the head of the household. I was just finishing my studies at the School of Architecture when I had to leave my mother, my brother, my girlfriend, my home. I was forced to do something unplanned, in the hope that better days lay ahead. Some of my friends had been mobilized. I feared being called up to fight a war which was not mine. I could not go and shoot at people just because they were of a different nationality, and because someone said they were our enemies. Besides, I had been taught that war is absurd.

I decided to leave home on 9 November 1991. The borders were closed at the time and that made my trip difficult. I had to travel through Macedonia to Bulgaria, then to Prague, and on to my final destination, London, where I stayed for four months. In London I worked as a dish-washer, a waiter and a pizza delivery courier. Unable to obtain a work permit and find the right job, I decided to go to Portugal, in the hope of finding work within my profession, architecture, as some of my friends had done. Once I got a job, I knew that my next step would be to complete my final year of study. Why?

— to link the practical experience I have acquired with the theoretical part that remains to be learned;

— to further my intellectual growth;

— to acquire a better position within my chosen profession;

— self-fulfilment;

— to be able to sign my own projects.

As a refugee from a country where a seemingly unending war is still raging, I cannot make long-term plans. The only thing I can plan right now is to get ahead professionally. I like Portugal as my second country, and for the time being I prefer to stay here. It is the only way I can help my retired mother in Belgrade. Still, I hope that the war in Yugoslavia will stop one day, and then I shall go back.

M. A.

Lisbon, Portugal

They Were Bitterly Disappointed

I left my country in June 1992 to avoid the draft. I wanted to go to Spain, where I had some friends, but I was turned back from the German border, and stayed in Austria. I was desperate at the time, and could not picture my future. But then I met some helpful people, to whom I am grateful for helping me find my way in Austria.

Ever since I left Yugoslavia I have tried to pursue my education. When I discovered that it was possible for foreign students to study in Austria, I took a preparatory German course at the University of Vienna. As one of the best students on the course, I was able to enrol at the university and enter student life.

Because of the political situation there, I do not expect to return to my country for the time being. On the other hand, I do not wish to become permanently settled in Austria. Once I have completed my studies, I would like to go back, when the situation there becomes normal again. A whole generation of young people has left Yugoslavia not because they do not believe in the future of that country, but because they were bitterly disappointed by current events. Being a part of that 'brain drain', I will postpone my return home until the present unfortunate situation improves. Under the present regime it is impossible to express one's opinions freely. All cultural and academic institutions are ideologically controlled by the ruling party.

In the meantime, the only goal I can achieve is to obtain the knowledge and skills necessary for me to become a useful member of a future Serbian society.

I. L.
Vienna, Austria

The United States and Me

I am about to begin a story about my past, about the country in which I was born, Bosnia, about cities, about life before and during the war, and about a new life here in the United States.

The plane left European soil on 23 February 1993. We refugees from Bosnia had left our country with a painful feeling of emptiness, emptiness because of the demolished cities, because of our homes which we had been thrown out of, and with a deep, deep sadness because of our sense of helplessness and inability to change our own reality. We were flying towards America. Some of us were naively delighted about the prospect of life in the Land of Opportunity. Some of us wept. I was wrapped up in thoughts of my own, but they were not very optimistic.

The next day we arrived in Houston, Texas. When I woke up, there, in Houston, I could not see the horizon. Only grey windows. And the sun outside. A lot of sunshine. When we left the plane, our faces were mercilessly exposed to the burning sun, and to a new life. I had never felt warmer in my life, or better.

But how did I end up in the United States? My father was a prisoner in the Serbian detention camps of Omarska and Manjaca. Along with him, all my family (mother, brother, sister and myself) were labelled 'victims of the civil war in Bosnia', which was another way of saying that we needed help and refuge, a secure place far away from the war. We came to the US by a decision of the US government and the International Migration Commissioner, to whom we are grateful for accepting us and giving us a chance to survive. Of course, I owe a big 'thank you' to this great country which made my first 'Good Morning' so good. I am grateful for being treated as a person, and not as a member of an ethnic group.

At the beginning, it was not easy to accept everything in this country. There was a culture shock because of the differences in tradition and lifestyle. The hugeness of the cities was fascinating. But the young adjust more easily, as did my sister, brother and I. For my parents it was different. They find their new life difficult, they feel as though everything has been a complete loss, a disaster. My parents do not speak English, which is their biggest problem. They are unable to find decent jobs, to communicate with their neighbours, to make new friends. And it is frustrating for both of them. My father, who was a civil engineer in Bosnia, now works packing groceries in a supermarket. My mother, who was a lawyer, is currently employed as a cleaner in a hotel. I would do anything to make their life easier and better, to see them happy again. The happiest moments for my parents are when they see the three of us smiling after passing our exams at school, because it is a sign of social recognition, which gives us some hope. Hope, after the inferno of the camps, after constant fear of death from shelling and sniper-fire.

I often think about how nice it would be to see my home in Bosnia just one more time, to see the old tree in front of our house, and the river… Pictures from my childhood, letters from my friends, memories of my family—they all make me remember the past. But I know that my wishes cannot come true, and that is what hurts so much. For the time being there is no chance of going back home. Especially since we Bosnians have been the victims of ethnic cleansing, a fact which erases every possibility and hope that I shall see Bosnia again soon. There are fewer and fewer Bosnians in Bosnia. The population has rapidly changed in the last years because of genocide. The very survival of the Bosnians is threatened. Methods of destruction and extermination have been invented and developed in comfortable rooms, perhaps even in the West. Meanwhile, the Bosnians have been waiting. Blindly, stupidly.

If I were in Bosnia, I would not be an avenger. I would not be capable of killing anybody. To deprive someone of life is to become as bestial as our enemies, who kill for no reason. There is no far-reaching solution to the war without the acceptance of differences and renewal of mutual tolerance. At least that is the gist of my microcosm of the world, a philosophy which may sound too utopian. But as long as I feel that way, I know that I can find tranquillity and peace within myself.

Everyone is capable of self-improvement if they work for it. That makes one more tolerant of others, and less aggressive.

In line with these ideas, my highest aim is to become a doctor. It is a hard task, and requires a lot of self-sacrifice. But I believe in myself. To me being a doctor means not only wearing a white coat, but also sharing the philosophy of altruism.

In real life, of course, even doctors are not born altruists. But, there *are* people who devote themselves to humanity. And I want to be one of them.

Right now, my real world is here in the US, in a country which offered me everything when I had nothing, no future, no hope, no self-confidence. Now I want to finish my education and gain some professional experience. I would like to be a useful member of the American community, and contribute to the development of my new homeland. Because I did not come here in pursuit of an education, but in search of a homeland.

However, I shall always be a proud Bosnian, because Bosnia is the most beautiful country I know. And I will continue to work voluntarily with the Refugee Service Alliance, helping refugees from all corners of the world to learn English, find jobs and feel at home again. I can see the possibility of going back to Bosnia sometime in the future, and I know that there are many Bosnians around the world who are still planning to return there. I want to do what I can to help those dreams come true.

A. H. A.
Houston, Texas, USA

Chapter 6: **Feelings of Deprivation**

A War Can't Be Just
If So Many Young People Die in It

I was born in 1971 in Belgrade, Yugoslavia. My parents are prominent journalists. Their professional practice is based on the fundamental principles of humanity and truth, and they raised me accordingly. Because of the nature of their work, they have many friends and colleagues of different nationalities and ethnic backgrounds. From an early age I was taught that colour, nationality and religious beliefs must never be criteria for my liking or disliking someone.

It was impossible for me even to imagine my Croatian or Bosnian friends as enemies, and I tried to say so. I took part in various protests and demonstrations against the Serbian government, because I thought that things would not have reached this point if the government had not been so concerned with its own selfish gains, which, in the long run, certainly had nothing to do with nationality, religion or, for that matter, democracy. But I still had my idea of a country in which we would all live together, building a better future (I thought no one would be so stupid as to destroy the beautiful country we had).

I started my university studies in Belgrade. I wanted to teach art history one day. Then the war started. It was impossible to imagine something so tragic and horrible, yet it was happening. More and more people sided with the nationalist government, proclaiming the war as just, because it was being fought for the freedom of all Serbs. I couldn't believe that people were actually accepting such nonsense as the truth. No war can be just if so many young people die in it. I was strongly opposed to the aims of this war, and could not believe it was happening, all the atrocities and crimes, neighbour against neighbour, brother against brother, man against man.

I had always declared myself a Yugoslav, but now, for the first time, I felt misplaced. I was ready to stand up for my beliefs and to try to save the idea of the old Yugoslavia in this new madness. But with every new day I had less and less strength to do so. Some of my friends were from Croatia, others from Bosnia. They began to receive threatening calls. One of them was killed somewhere in Croatia, others went into hiding. Belgrade became a dangerous place. 'You too can be powerful—just pick up a gun' became the new slogan. People like me, who believed in all nationalities and religions living in one democratic and free country, made themselves scarce. They were afraid to express their views. My greatest disappointment was the peace movement which, at its biggest rally, only managed to assemble about two hundred people. I couldn't believe that people were seeing all these crimes, all these young men dying, and so few were willing to try to do something about it.

The last year that I was at the University of Belgrade, I finally came to the conclusion that nobody could do anything for anyone, that even the students, who were supposed to be progressive in their way of thinking, did not believe strongly enough in the political struggle. My studies have much to do with history, and I have become aware of strange twists in historiography. History teaches us that things were not always as they were supposed to be, but as a particular ideology wanted them to be. When one of my best professors, a prominent historian and leader of an opposition party, left the country, I finally realized that it was time to go. I didn't feel safe. I felt constant pressure to join the crazed masses, and more and more often I was called a traitor, stupid, cowardly, unpatriotic, by people who used to be my friends. I went to the UK, and after some time I found a university that suited me. Now I study classical civilization and history. I have always been interested in all aspects of history, especially the influence of a civilization on its environment and on other cultures. I think that one can better understand the present if one knows more about the past.

When I finish my studies, I wish to return to Belgrade to teach younger generations about the true meaning of history, not as it is taught now, with nationalist overtones. The importance of Athenian democracy and its impact on today's world must not be overlooked. Democracy is something you cherish and protect, not something you take for granted. In war-torn Yugoslavia, democracy has to be taught all over again, and this time the right way. I hope that I shall be one of the new teachers for a new generation.

M. J.
London, UK

Few Expectations
of the First Days of Independence
Have Been Fulfilled

In 1992 I was a student of psychology at Zagreb University. I had great plans. I was deeply discontented with the situation at the university and with the political situation in Croatia.

At the university it was chaos. The criteria for academic achievement did not seem to matter any more. Students who had taken part in defending the country, and were able to provide some sort of proof, could get credits for courses they never actually attended. Quite a number of students forged their papers, and that opened the door to corruption. Others did not sit their exams because of 'depression brought on by the stress of war', and that was tolerated. Although I respect the defenders of our country, I still think the university should promote academic criteria above all else.

The political atmosphere in Croatia was equally discouraging. Eruptions of nationalism grew and multiplied through the war. Those who had seen the tragedy of the first independent state of Croatia (1941–45) became anxious. The Croatian government began to adopt a more and more authoritarian style, borrowing phrases and slogans from the old communist brand of populism. Few expectations of the first days of independence have been fulfilled.

I am a Croat, but I have Austrian and Jewish ancestors as well. Multicultural and multiethnic societies have always seemed very natural to me. Unfortunately, during this war and because of it, many people lost faith in such a society, which had been one of the most precious ideals of all progressive-minded people, especially in the former multicultural Yugoslavia. I write this without any nostalgia for the old Yugoslavia. My idea is of several closely linked multiethnic countries with good relations. This is the only way I can envisage the whole region within the context of a united Europe.

All the unhappy events in my country, coupled with painful personal problems (my family lived through the war in Slavonia), affected me so much that I lapsed into a prolonged state of deep apathy.

In the spring of 1992, with the best recommendations from my professors, I applied for one of ten scholarships granted by the Austrian government. And I had the honour of being selected. That is how I came to study in Vienna.

Although I take a rather critical view of the situation at home, I have to emphasize that I love my country. I think it is one of the most beautiful places in the world, and its people are warm and friendly. I am sure it is where I belong.

R. K.

Vienna, Austria

In the Winds of Corruption and Poverty

I was born in Belgrade, Yugoslavia. In the summer of 1990 I came to the USA for the first time as an eight-week visitor at the world famous Interlochen Center for the Arts, in Michigan. I applied to Interlochen as a composition major and was accepted with a half-tuition scholarship in piano and music theory.

I cannot say that I planned to apply to a university in the US, but in the end I gave it a try. Three weeks later I received a letter from the director of the DePauw University School of Music, stating that I was being considered for a full-tuition scholarship for their undergraduate programme, which I was subsequently offered. I went back to Yugoslavia to finish high school. I was not sure whether to go to the US or stay at home, because I had been accepted at the Music Academy of Belgrade as a conducting major.

During the 1991–92 academic year the political and economic situation in Yugoslavia worsened and became both unpredictable and unpromising. In the meantime I stayed in touch with DePauw University, which offered to defer my scholarship until the following year. Considering the rapidly changing political situation in my country, I did not have much time to make up my mind.

My 1991–92 academic year was very successful. I became assistant conductor with Collegium Musicum, the Belgrade Music Academy Women's Choir, and assistant conductor with Branko Krsmanović, the Belgrade University Mixed Choir, which had a high reputation worldwide. We toured France, Belgium, Greece and Austria. I did well in all the exams at the academy, but the educational conditions became harder and harder, and at moments almost impossible. Classes were held irregularly, and towards the end of the school year rarely. Life turned into a daily struggle for survival. My father, like many others, was suspended from his job. At the end of May 1992, when I was about to take my final exams, anti-war demonstrations started at all universities in the Federal Republic of Yugoslavia. I took part in them, which gave me an opportunity to reconsider my own situation. The demonstrations lasted for several weeks, and were cruelly put down by the government. The university was closed. I knew that something very wrong was happening, but I could do nothing about it. I felt desperate. My friends were being dragged into a war they did not want to fight. Everything was falling apart. The intelligentsia of my country were fighting one another, contradicting themselves. Most young people wanted to support democracy, but there were few democratic forces to support. Their parents, meanwhile, were blinded by the blaze of the war.

I realized that the only way to become a productive part of society was to do what one does best. But that was not easy, because education, and culture as a whole, were the first to collapse in the winds of corruption and poverty. For me the only thing to do was to accept the scholarship at DePauw University and continue my education there. I was on the waiting list for the Prague–Chicago flight for three weeks. And then one morning at 8 a.m. a lady from the travel agency called to tell me that there was finally a seat for me on the plane, and that the bus for Prague was leaving that evening. I did not have much time to say goodbye to my parents.

S. A.

Greencastle, Indiana, USA

Feelings of Deprivation and Helplessness

I must admit that I find it very hard to write this essay: how is one supposed to reveal all the things that have haunted one for the past couple of years—to perfect strangers, however friendly they may be? That would be too painful, and take too long, I thought at first. But when I mentioned it to a friend, she lifted her eyebrows and said:

'You are supposed to write it in one or two pages? That's way too much; you can give all your reasons in a single curse.'

Of course, I am not going to lay bare my memories, and I am certainly not going to be uncivil. There are many reasons for my leaving my 'former homeland'—emotional, existential, intellectual—but they are all epitomized in two feelings I have had for a long time: deprivation and helplessness.

Three years ago when I left Sarajevo to study at Belgrade University, it seemed like a good start to my new 'adult' life and college education. It was the only university in the former Yugoslavia to offer such an extensive combined academic programme in Yugoslav and comparative literature. I thought I could have not chosen better. I did not see the war coming, and I was naive enough to laugh away all the bad things happening around me. But when I realized how easily reason could be overwhelmed by nationalist propaganda and claustrophobia, I stopped laughing.

Not long after the start of the war in Bosnia, Belgrade University lost its autonomy, and its students were deprived of their right to shape their studies and future. It was not long before the Department of Yugoslav Literature became the Department of Serbian Literature and Language. Some of the professors found it convenient to change the concept of their lectures to fit the claustrophobic title of the programme. (Whether that decision was made out of fear or conviction did not alter the final outcome.) In order to do this they had to withhold certain information from their students, otherwise it would be obvious that Serbian literature is not an organic form unto itself, without reference to and interaction with other Yugoslav literature. What had been good guidance in our critical readings and theoretical and historical knowledge during my first year of studies turned into a more or less successful personal search in Belgrade's libraries for a 'second opinion'.

I could not but despise those of my professors who placed their reputations in the service of nationalist propaganda. I could not but pity those who kept their minds open, and felt as desperate and deprived as I did. Neither contempt nor pity is a feeling that should be generated by the people who are supposed to be guiding our college (and all other) education. It was impossible really to study (or really live, for that matter) without being given a choice of different views, without being part of the cultural and social polyphony of life.

And since I had come to Belgrade from Sarajevo, and with my parents still there at the time, I could not help thinking that it was as if those of my professors who were crazed with nationalism were themselves firing guns at my parents and destroying my native town.

You would like to know something about my plans for the future. During this war I have felt helpless and scared, unable to control my own private life, let alone anything more, deprived—like every ex-Yugoslav—of the right to plan my future. I do not dare to think about the future of anyone who has had an experience similar to mine. Our fears and wounds have to be healed. If there is a chance for that (and there must be), all I can say is that I shall be proud to be part of it, and shall contribute as much as I can.

My favourite poem of the past couple of years ends with the lines:

> Homeless is thy sorrow, mute thy word,
> Terrified of conviction for not being able
> to do a thing.

Czeslaw Milosz

S. K.
London, UK

The Opposition Was Weak, Almost Invisible

I finished high school in Belgrade, Yugoslavia, in June 1989 and enrolled at Belgrade University in October of that same year, majoring in philosophy. At the same time I worked for the media, mainly for B-92, the independent radio station.

As the 1990–91 academic year approached, the economic and political situation in the country worsened. The economic reform collapsed, and with it so did my financial resources. My parents were no longer able to support me. I decided to continue my education abroad. The United Kingdom was my first choice, because of my fluent English, and my interest in social anthropology, a field in which British universities are very strong. I applied to the London School of

Economics and was admitted. I graduated from LSE with second class (upper division) honours in June 1994. I was also awarded the LSE Michael Sallnow Prize for the best final year essay in anthropology: my topic was the European 'understanding' of indigenous art and a comparative study of various applicable philosophical, sociological and anthropological theories.

But my reasons for leaving Yugoslavia were not limited to my interest in social anthropology alone. As I have already mentioned, I had worked for an independent radio station, and openly declared myself to be a member of the Serbian political opposition, which was weak and almost invisible at the time. Having courageously broadcast critical programmes and interviews, the radio station soon became a thorn in the side of the regime. During the summer of 1990, I realized that the cause for which we were fighting might soon prove to be a lost one. We were not allowed to broadcast freely, we were not given a broadcasting frequency, which meant we were broadcasting as a pirate radio station. As differences between my radio station and the ruling party and regime grew, my position became more and more difficult. Besides, my family became increasingly worried about my future in Belgrade. So I left.

It would be arrogant to say that I feel like a political refugee. That is not the case. I was not directly persecuted, nor was I harassed by the regime. That would certainly be an overstatement. But the truth is that I felt increasingly unsafe and, even more than that, disappointed by what was being achieved by my radio station, and other opposition-oriented media, in their struggle against a totalitarian socialist regime. I felt I could be more helpful if I went abroad to continue my education at a distinguished foreign university, and to be a UK correspondent at a time when the media blockade was already quite strong and it was hard to obtain impartial information from abroad.

The link between anthropology and the media can be a very fruitful field of research. The war in Yugoslavia, however horrible it is, is becoming an increasingly interesting field of research for sociologists, anthropologists and media researchers. It is a war at the end of the twentieth century and, beyond any doubt, it is also a media war. Media influence on developing and broadening this conflict is vast, and worth studying. This is my point of departure in my MA on media and communications research at the LSE.

N. D.

London, UK

I Started to Lose All Hope of a Better Life

I was born in Split, Croatia, which was then a part of Yugoslavia. My mother is a Croat, my father a Montenegrin. They both came from families where no one had ever paid much attention to nationality. That was the way I was brought up.

But when I was still a baby, a nationalist movement developed in Croatia, and my parents had to leave Split, because the local people began to threaten them. (They used to reproach my grandmother for 'keeping Serbs in her house'.) Since then we have lived in Belgrade.

When the political situation began to get complicated once again, I felt that insisting on the 'national question' was just an excuse for keeping absolute control over the people and undermining the process of opening the country up to Europe and the world, a process which had begun under Ante Marković's government. The hunger for unlimited power after the fall of communism was most easily satisfied by mobilizing people to fight for the so-called national cause, while monopolizing the economy and maintaining the status quo.

I attended opposition party rallies regularly. But soon I realized that they were changing their political platforms in order to gain more votes. From a liberal, anti-war policy they turned right-wing, accusing the government of not being tough enough in dealing with Serbian territorial and national interests. As for political life in Serbia, I do not believe that any of the current programmes, be they pro-socialist, pro-capitalist, pro-republican or pro-monarchist, can solve the problem.

I took part in most of the opposition's demonstrations, but after a while I gave up. I witnessed the humiliation of people from other parts of the former Yugoslavia, especially from Croatia and Bosnia, just because their family names were not Serbian, and I realized that people were losing their jobs for the same reason, that they had to flee abroad to save their lives, and that no one could help them, no one really cared. I started to lose all hope for a better life in my country. Every time I wanted to express my views or raise some questions, at the university or in the street, I was accused of selling out the eternal interests of the Serbian people, of ignoring the great Vatican-CIA-Arab plot against them, of being a traitor and, worst of all—of being a Croat.

I left the country on 18 June 1992, together with my sister, who had the same problems and the same convictions as I had. We chose the UK because we had learned English at school, and we have friends there.

Now I am a student of civil engineering at the University of Westminster, and my dream is to go back to Yugoslavia, when it becomes a democratic country, which I know it will be one day, because it is the only natural way to go, and nothing can stop it from happening. The country has great potential and good prospects once this horrible war is over. But it will need not only economic and political recovery, but also cultural revival, because so many educated people, scientists and artists, have left. The same thing happened some fifty years ago, and the country was rebuilt from scratch. And so it will be again.

K. V.
London, UK

There Was Nothing I Could Meaningfully Do in My Country

When the crisis in Yugoslavia really began I was at the end of my history of art studies at the University of Belgrade (Serbia). At the time I was one of the editors of the monthly review *Views*, which specialized in cultural matters and advocated an end to authoritarianism and stronger cultural links with modern Europe. I was also active in the opposition movement.

When it became clear that war was imminent, and when the army sent call-up papers to my house, I left the country, refusing to take part in a war against young men whom I had hitherto considered my fellow-countrymen, a war characterized by cruelty and wanton destruction. This was not what I had had in mind when I had done my regular army service several years earlier. There was nothing I could meaningfully do in Serbia: the publisher of *Views* and other editors had already left.

After a stay in Czechoslovakia and in Norway I came to Canterbury as a training fellow in modern cultural studies at the University of Kent.

The fact that I did not respond to repeated summonses to do my military duty makes me a draft resister. Appeals to the parliament of the 'new' Yugoslavia, controlled by the Socialist Party and the fascist Radical Party, to declare an amnesty for those who refused to take part in the war, were rejected with angry statements that such 'traitors' must be punished. I have not applied for asylum, believing that the regime in Serbia will not last forever, and I do not want to sever my links with my country and culture.

Residing abroad, I suffer legally from the fact that I am considered a citizen of the Federal Republic of Yugoslavia, which has generally not been recognized and is subject to international sanctions. As a result, I cannot use any intergovernmental arrangements for studies and scholarships. When my citizenship does not weigh against me, then it is my ethnic background: the general stereotype of the cruel, genocidal Serb is a difficult burden to bear—an average newspaper reader does not know that any opposition even exists in Serbia.

The disastrous policies of the Serbian regime and international sanctions endanger the spiritual existence of the Serbian nation. I believe that the best thing I can do is to work hard on my education so as to be of some assistance when I go back. I have stayed in touch with the Department of Philosophy in Belgrade, which is now functioning under extremely difficult circumstances (lack of new books, periodicals, links with kindred institutions abroad, etc.). The impression I have after speaking to some of the professors and lecturers there is one of encouragement to continue my studies abroad and become some kind of link between these two, at the moment, separate worlds. My ambition is to go back to Yugoslavia and try to use the knowledge and experience I have acquired in Great Britain to help the cultural renewal of my unfortunate country.

Lately I have been active in the campaign launched by the European Civic Forum to support deserters and draft resisters from the former Yugoslavia. One of the aspects of this campaign is to help those young people from the former Yugoslavia who have interrupted their studies because of the war. In October 1993 the European Parliament adopted a resolution on deserters from the armed forces of states in the former Yugoslavia. The significance of this resolution (so far only on paper) is enormous: point six calls upon member states to develop programmes and projects which seek to provide possibilities for training or further education for deserters and draft resisters. So far the Open Society Grant Program has been a rare opportunity to fulfil this aim.

B. D.

Canterbury, UK

Human Life Deserves Much More Than to Be Erased By the Whistle of a Bullet

A couple of days ago I unexpectedly came across an application form for the Open Society Institute Supplementary Grant Program. I couldn't believe that this world still cares about the citizens of the former Yugoslavia who have left their country, convinced that war is no way to settle disputes between people.

I was born in 1969. My parents raised me as a true Yugoslav, but most of all they taught me to respect people for who they are, not for the group they belong to. I enjoyed travelling all over Yugoslavia and admired its beauties. No matter where I was—in the lake district of Plitvice, in the caves of Postojna, in the canyon of the River Tara or on the beaches of Lake Ohrid—I felt at home. In the first twenty years of my life everything was nice and easy. After high school I was accepted into medical school, fulfilling my dream. After finishing my military service I went to medical school where I discovered the awesome world of medicine. I studied with enthusiasm and did very well in my exams. Everything in my life seemed perfect. I had a girlfriend I loved, many friends I could trust, a lot of acquaintances, and great expectations of the future, which didn't seem hard to realize.

But then came the summer of 1991. I watched in disbelief the TV reports of fighting between the Yugoslav Army and the local population in Slovenia. I hoped it was only a temporary crisis, and that everything would soon be as it was before. Then the conflict spread to Croatia. Still, I didn't attach too much importance to it, because I strongly believed that the common people would not let themselves be pushed into a war for the sick ambitions of their politicians. I was wrong. The people of Yugoslavia were cheated and manipulated by strong government propaganda. In the autumn of 1991 there was intensive mobilization in Belgrade. Like many of my friends, I did not want to go to war. I avoided my house, and slept at my uncle's. However, at the beginning of November the military authorities started looking for me more often. With the blessing and support of my family I decided to leave Yugoslavia. The initial plan was to stay a couple of months in Canada until the madness subsided. I am still waiting for that to happen.

My arrival in Canada has been marked by my efforts to start a new life and by the many difficulties I have had to overcome in order to survive and adapt to a new culture and environment. But I have never questioned my decision to leave Yugoslavia. I did not want to be a part of that collective madness. I don't dare to think what would have happened had I taken part in the killings. I think I would prefer to be shot dead than to live with the images of horror that would haunt me for the rest of my life. I do not believe in war as a means for dealing with social problems. And I do not need it to create my own niche in society. I believe I have other qualities. Human life deserves much more than to be erased by the whistle of a bullet or the explosion of a mortar shell. Of course, I would have fought if my country had been invaded from outside, and if my family and people had been in danger. However, I did not want to let a communist regime toy with my life. I had different plans for my future, and I did not want to waste the only life I have for nothing. There are many people I love and care about, and I decided to carry on living for their sake. I want to save myself for better times. If I were in Belgrade right now, I would probably give up under the pressure of media propaganda. It sends out all sorts of information to the small human brain, gradually forcing it to lose its rationality and independence of thought. This process weakens the rational mechanism which enables us to distinguish between good and evil, the reasonable and the unreasonable. The media thus become the means for directing thoughts and emotions into the human skull.

Canada offered me refuge and support in fulfilling my dreams. I am working towards my goal of becoming a doctor, but most of all I am working on myself as a human being. Right now I am in the third year of the chemistry programme, and hopefully in September 1995 I will be back on track as a medical student.

Although I am happy here in Canada, and I have become a relatively successful member of the community, my future plans are geared towards Yugoslavia. I feel that it is my responsibility to help my anguished nation to forget quickly this unfortunate war, and to regain its lost pride and good reputation.

Lj. I.
Toronto, Canada

How the Media Can Be Misused

I left the former Yugoslavia and continued my education abroad for reasons of personal academic interest and because of the situation in my country.

I was fourteen when I wrote my first article for the school newspaper. Ever since, my main academic interest has been communication and images of contemporary society, the process of their creation and their impact on our lives.

Classes in journalism, the culture of communication, and sociology at secondary school, together with work experience in the media, have been of enormous importance to me in understanding these issues. However, the impact the media (especially the state media) had on provoking and encouraging war and hate among the people of the former Yugoslavia made me aware of how the media can be misused, and to what tragic ends. As far as I can remember, it was on television that Croats first heard that they hated Serbs.

I felt despair watching the local news, which so obviously lacked any impartiality and objectivity. We found that British, German and American radio stations and satellite TV channels offered more accurate reports. Croatian Television would sometimes show reports made by CNN, the BBC, etc., minus the parts that were considered 'anti-Croat'.

My frustration with the situation and my interest in the mass media led me to look for a university course which would teach me how the media can be used responsibly. No such course existed in Croatia. But excellent results in my final exams at secondary school and fluency in English enabled me to apply to British universities.

The course I attend, communication and image studies at the University of Kent in Canterbury, is unique in the world in that its content and critical approach go beyond simple communication studies. It has proved to be exactly what I hoped for. I am already able to see much more clearly how the media work, both at the technological and at the ideological level. By the end of this course, I think I shall have enough academic and practical knowledge to work in the media, providing as accurate information as possible.

Many journalists in Croatia risked their lives reporting from the front lines. Many others put themselves in the service of a repressive, harmful ideology. Reports by foreign organizations such as Amnesty International and Helsinki Watch showed that the Croatian media have a long way to go before Croatia can rightfully claim to be a democratic country. However, I don't see the situation in my country as hopeless. There are a few independent magazines, radio and TV stations, which try to give a fair picture of what is happening. My work experience has mostly been with them.

What I would like to do when I finish my course is to go back to Croatia and continue working for media organizations which are not mere instruments of the ruling party. I think I shall be able to do so because I have kept up my contacts with them through occasional contributions. I would like to work for Croatian Television, which by then, I hope and believe, will be on its way to becoming a democratic medium. Its importance and influence are enormous and it is therefore essential that it should work according to Western standards of reporting. I would like to contribute to this transformation by applying the academic and work experience I have gained here in Britain. I would also like to bring with me the sense of tolerance and respect for different points of view that I have learned from people here.

A. S.

Canterbury, UK

Now I Have Friends Fighting in Four Different Armies

Why did I leave? The answer is pretty obvious, one might say, but different people have different points of departure.

Quite a while before the war actually started, a lot of my friends and I felt increasingly uneasy about the way things were developing in our country. After the first run of 'free' elections in Croatia, Slovenia and Serbia, the stage was more or less set for war. It was quite obvious that it would be very difficult to remain impartial and sane under the pressure of the media, friends and family—so I decided to leave as soon as the opportunity arose.

I first tried Greece where I had some friends, but as my hope of finding a job there failed, I returned home. Finally, on 29 August 1991, I left for Germany and then for Great Britain. My last weeks at home were chaotic and confusing: a schoolfriend of mine who was on the same coach for Munich said he just couldn't stand all those flags being hoisted everywhere, and that seems to sum it all up.

The nonsense of the nationalist arguments being hurled at everyone from all sides made it impossible for me to fight in a war that was just beginning when I left. I could not see myself fighting on either of the sides involved, and I could not accept the line of 'defending the country' that was being force-fed to everyone. I was sure it was the corrupt politicians who were to blame for the war, and I certainly did not want to fight for their cause.

Some of my friends who opposed the warmongering stayed on to 'face the music', and continued their work either by joining opposition parties or by choosing the civil service option while serving in the military—whatever army it may have been. Now I have friends (or former friends) fighting in (or dodging) at least four different armies (factions). I did not want to do that because I was too weak at the time—I had serious problems with inexplicable attacks of fatigue, and mentally I was utterly confused: I knew things were wrong, but I did not know what to do about the madness around me.

H. L.
London, UK

I Couldn't Take It Any More

'I am a Yugoslav from Belgrade. And let's get something straight: I am not the product of a mixed marriage, that's not why I feel Yugoslav. I am a Yugoslav by conviction...'

These are the opening lines of an article I wrote for the news magazine *Nin*, just after I left the country. The article was called: 'A Letter from Holland'. My friend B.I. had asked me to write an article about my reasons for leaving because that was around the time that Belgraders were starting to realize that a lot of young people had already left the country. It was a slightly pathetic letter, but it was honest, it was an attempt to speak out against the national madness that had taken hold of my country. When the article was published, my friends in Belgrade started phoning me, asking what gave me the right to appear in the papers, saying I should be ashamed of having run away, of being a traitor...

Traitor. The word often crops up in my own lengthy ponderings about why I left. A traitor, yes, but to what? Do you have the right to betray your country when it steps knee-deep into the boots of fascism? Do you have the right to remain true to your ideals which can be compressed into a single word: tolerance? And to what extent do you have the right to protest against what is happening in your country if you have already decided to leave it?

I am obsessed with these questions and every day I try to find answers to them. Even now in these few sentences I am trying to explain why I really left Yugoslavia. The answer is very simple: I couldn't take it any more.

I couldn't take having to cope every day with the intoxication of people around me who had finally 'seen the light', something I couldn't see at all. I couldn't take the terrible feeling of helplessness and of being unable to change anything. I couldn't go on fighting the monsters of the past, distorted history and lies. I couldn't take it any more.

Maybe that makes me a weak man, ill-prepared to face the reality of fascism. The only way I knew how to fight was by means of civil resistance, because I strongly believed that a state based on civil rights is the only solution for the unfortunate Yugoslav peoples. I left when I realized that civil resistance to nationalism is impossible. Nationalists don't listen, they shoot.

For a long time I was plagued by a feeling of guilt, because, in the final analysis, who can bring about the changes I so desperately want if not people like me? Perhaps I should have stayed. I started secretly admiring people who had made a different choice: to fight from within. Trying to find an answer to the problems, I exchanged long letters with B.I., a man who had decided not to leave. And then one day he wrote and said: 'Eventually it will probably become impossible to live here. Meanwhile, we "opponents" are putting up a fight, each in our own way, aware that under conditions like these and with a nation like this, we won't be enough of a factor to turn things around. However it may look to you from where you are, there is nothing heroic about our "struggle". How can you be any kind of hero under conditions like these?' A few months ago my friend left Belgrade and is now living in Italy.

His words helped me to find a way to fight. I realized that I can do much more from here, that here I have far greater possibilities to renew my contacts with friends from 'enemy' parts of the former Yugoslavia. I realized that leaving had been my own decision and that it does not stop me, that it actually helps me to continue to 'fight'. The unheroic way. The civil way.

Then I launched a paper called *BEODAM*, and I began studying hard. Because in some strange, inexplicable way, I see every good grade as a small victory for democracy, proof that something can be done, in spite of everything.

Do I want to go back to Yugoslavia? Quite honestly, that's all I do want. But not to this kind of Yugoslavia, where Mr Željko Ražnjatović-Arkan, a man who is wanted by Interpol and who is on the list of international war criminals, sits in parliament. Not to a

Yugoslavia which wages an undeclared war. Not to a Yugoslavia which does not recognize the rights of national minorities. Sorry, I don't feel Serb enough for that.

I will do my utmost to go back to Yugoslavia. To Yugoslavia as a civil state which respects the rights of minorities, to a democratic state which lives in peace with its neighbours. I will do my utmost to see the birth of such a Yugoslavia. I will fight for it, but I will continue to do so unheroically, the civil way. It's the only way I know.

$\overline{V.\ I.}$

Amsterdam, Holland

That's Why I Left Everything

The second Yugoslavia, which encompassed six republics, several nations and nationalities of different religions and cultural and political persuasions, violently disintegrated in mid-1991. The war that began then continues unabated to this day, with slim prospects of soon ending peacefully (by 'peacefully' I mean by political and diplomatic means, through dialogue). The entire region of the former Yugoslavia and all its peoples who now live in their own separate little states have been set back in every respect. The reputation of this once universally acknowledged country has been torn to shreds. It is hard to contemplate the future when the present is so dismal.

The year 1991, when the entire Eastern socialist bloc collapsed, brought Yugoslavia the possibility of deciding its future and fate in a new, democratic way. For the first time people were able to take part in genuine democratic elections, with real choices. The problem, in my opinion, was the absence of an interim period, a psychological pause. Everything happened too quickly and once again the basic, starting idea was badly implemented. Instead of constructive options, which would have ensured peace and prosperity, destructive options won out, as a result of which we now have hardly any future at all.

1991 was a humiliating year for everyone who upheld, in mind and in deed, the idea of a democratic, open society on the Karl Popper model. Crudeness increased by the day and the gap between the lead-ing political elites and the man in the street widened. Along with the violent conflicts being waged on our doorstep (conflicts we didn't want and didn't support), fear crept into our hearts—fear not that we would be killed, but that we would have to kill! To kill on the threshold of the 21st century? I could not agree to kill or to help those who were doing the killing, whatever their reason! It is not exactly easy to live in a country at war and to know that everything could have been and still could be different.

For all these reasons, and because I am opposed to any kind of violence, in November 1991 I left Belgrade, Yugoslavia, my family, my friends, everything I had. I set out (as I told my friends) in search of a life worth living. I am currently living and studying in a country which pays far greater attention to the elementary needs, rights and liberties of the individual. I am completely satisfied with my studies in philosophy and Slavistics, but I am sorry that I had to travel so far to gain the minimum conditions essential for a healthy and normal life!

I think (and hope) that my future will be part of our joint future. Yugoslavia as a country is no longer what it once was. Many parts of the former Yugoslavia have been completely destroyed and devastated. People have been massacred. Survivors are forced to carry on in the hope that one day they will see better times. But peace, like war, does not come of itself. Essential though they are, individual efforts are not enough. Joint initiatives are the only way to exert a positive, more decisive influence in this situation of overwhelming chaos. Someone has to put out the fire ignited by negligence and ignorance. Someone has to rebuild what has been destroyed. We all have to make sure that our own terrible experience is never repeated again. And there lies my future. I've already had some experience in the fields of culture and communication. I would like to work in the media (journalism), but still lack the conditions for doing so. To my great regret I haven't yet found a circle of people who share my views and outlook. When I graduate I will most probably return home and try to pass on all the things I have learned here in Germany, to rebuild the bridges that once connected us with the rest of the world. I hope that our joint efforts will finally bear fruit and that we will create a 'just' peace, which will serve as a stable foundation for generations to come.

A. M.
Tübingen, Germany

Why Is the World So Unfair to Us ?

I am Albanian. I come from Ferizaj, Kosova. I was born in a poor village. My family is poor. I grew up watching members of my family do really hard manual work. The village is located next to mountains, with a quarry nearby. The villagers have to work hard to earn their living and daily bread. I began to think that the Albanian people were cursed, and wondered how long this would continue.

My father worked as a teacher in the village school. I would ask him sometimes what was happening around us. There were things I saw on TV and heard on the radio. He would pretend not to hear what I was asking, or would urge me to go outside and play with the other village children. Although I was a little boy, I was curious to find out why we were so poor and so unlucky. There was a Serbian family living in our village and their children had some expensive, nice toys. Again, I kept asking myself why the world was so unfair to us. Winter would come, and my father would go to the nearby mountain to get logs for the fire, to keep us warm. I would wait for him, sitting next to my grandfather. I kept asking lots of questions, and he would respond by saying that I was only a little boy and could not understand the real reasons why the world was the way it was. The time came for me to go to school. I remember my teacher as a very devoted person, and my classes were very interesting, especially reading and the Albanian language. I was one of the best students in the class. My teacher kept encouraging me to study harder and harder. Life went on. I passed the second grade, and the third. And with the help of my father I managed to attend high school, which I enjoyed a lot.

But I was faced with tremendous difficulties. The school was divided into two camps: the Albanian and the Serb. We Albanians were harassed in every possible way. On one occasion, when we were protesting against government measures which treated Albanian students unfairly, the Serbian police used poisonous gas against us. More than six thousand students were affected by it. But life went on. I was just about to finish school, when one day I received a letter from the recruitment office, informing me that I was registered as a new recruit of the Yugoslav People's Army. Aware that many Albanians came home dead from their compulsory military service, I decided to avoid conscription and flee to Tirana, where I wanted to continue my education.

Now I am twenty years old. I study pharmacy. But I keep wondering whether there will be a time when I will enjoy life in my homeland. I am studying here as a second-year student, in the hope of a brighter future. I am pursuing my studies in a field which has always interested me. It is the human side of my profession which interests me. I want to alleviate the suffering of my people to the extent that I can. This keeps me going.

Although I am living away from home, my thoughts often return to Kosova, where I grew up and where my family live. I dare not go there right now, as my life might be in danger. But I intend to go one day. The Albanian people of Kosova continue their struggle for survival. They have been challenging the Serbian regime, showing them that they will never give up. That spirit keeps me going and makes me more optimistic about the future. I hope that prosperity and happiness are not far away.

May God help us.

———

T. K.
Tirana, Albania

The Chances I Was Looking for
Were Not There Either

For my generation of Albanian high school kids there was no place to hide from the Serbian military police. As soon as we finished school, they called us up for compulsory military service, which would nowadays mean fighting on the front lines against Croats or Bosnians. Since my primary goal was to be healthy, i.e. to stay alive, and to study, I had no choice but to leave home. In Kosova I would have been unable to do either: the University of Kosova was closed down by the Serbs in 1989, and in the army I might have been wounded or killed somewhere in Croatia.

I now live in Vienna. In September 1991 I left Kosova and went to Zagreb, where after two months I managed only to obtain a pass to go to Istanbul, Turkey. There I stayed three months, only to find that the opportunities I was looking for were not there either. From Turkey I went to Switzerland, where I stayed fourteen months as a refugee/deserter. This ultimately led me to apply to the Technical University of Vienna. I have been studying computer science in Vienna since 1993. My one goal is to obtain my university degree. Although I want to go back home, that, unfortunately, is not possible at the present time. The political future is uncertain. Of course, I am confident that the time will come when I will be able to return home, together with all my fellow Kosovans. When it comes, I shall be ready to help rebuild our country.

B. F.
Vienna, Austria

Chapter 7: **In Search of Identity**

The Thread That Binds Me

I saw the Danube again, for the first time in two years. It was the same—dark, lazy, seemingly indifferent. It still had that same old smell, that old monotonous rhythm, that same cold touch to the fingertips, that same taste on my lips. I closed my eyes, confused by the rush of feelings touched off by this sluggish ash-grey river. It was so wonderful to be in Novi Sad again.

'So, what was so wonderful about it?' a friend of mine asked, a few months later, as we sat in a café in Tel Aviv, while the sun sank behind a horizon that overlooked some other water, filling me with a wave of nostalgia. I know, it's hard for an outsider to understand that you can find anything wonderful in a country devastated by war, sanctions and poverty. And what does the word 'wonderful' mean, anyway? Perhaps it's not the best word. It was strange, sad, moving, interesting, pleasant, unique... All of it untranslatable into words, as elusive as a morning dream, as unclear as the start of a smile at the corner of someone's mouth, as sad as the closing titles of a favourite movie. How can I explain this blur of different images, newspaper clippings, TV newsreels, wads of worthless money with astronomical figures, and all the queues, queues and more queues. So much unhappiness and poverty in one place, such despair and bitterness in people's hearts, so many shattered dreams and lives... And so much anger and hatred in people's souls, tearful eyes with questioning or accusing looks, in which the last ray of hope is fading. And always those damned, omnipresent questions: 'Did it have to be like this?' 'What now?' 'What next?'... Like a nightmare that slowly turns into the reality of day.

Sitting on the sand in the shadow of the bridge, I could feel my illusions slowly slipping through my open fingers, disappearing into the ashen whirlpool of my river, along with millions of other, similar illusions probably… I had already pulled my anchor out of that mud, and I had no desire to toss it back in again.

The day of my departure was sad. Sad like the two old people standing in the street, waving goodbye until their silhouettes were blurred by the tears in my eyes: grey like the bus driver who was taking me far away; wretched like the people who had already formed queues in front of the still unopened banks and supermarkets; weary like the city which kept silent while the autumn wind lashed out at it; empty somehow, like me, because I was leaving a part of me behind.

Sometimes, when I look out from my university building and over the dazzling white stone of Jerusalem, over all those hills and forests, over the ramparts of the old city and the golden cupola I had once seen only in pictures, I'm glad I'm here. I feel that this is where I should be. And when I close my eyes I hear the river murmur a lullaby to the city on its banks, and I see the moon's reflection in it, shimmering at the foot of the fortress. And it is then that I feel the thread that binds me to Yugoslavia, a thread that sooner or later will pull me there. Sooner or later, whether for a few days, months, years, or my whole life, I don't know. But I do know it will happen. In peacetime, I hope, in better times.

R. K.
Jerusalem, Israel

A Story of Lost Identity

Three years ago I was living the life I wanted. And then my country was torn apart by political and national conflict. My father is a Croat, my mother a Serb. I was supposed to be a Croat. We lived in Belgrade, the capital of Serbia. When the war broke out, anyone who had any links with Croatia, or was a Croat, was threatened, physically and mentally mistreated. Many lost their jobs, like my father, although he had been very successful in his work.

I dared not mention my national origin at school. But then questionnaires were introduced into all schools, asking students about their place of birth, their nationality, where their parents were from, etc.

Under 'Nationality' I wanted to say: 'Yugoslav', but it was not allowed.

Life became more and more unbearable for me and my family. We thought about moving to Croatia, because my father had no chance of finding another job in Belgrade. There was also the danger that he might be called up to fight against his own people. So we were forced to run away to Croatia. But our life in Croatia was no better. Because of my mother. Since she is a Serb there was no chance of her getting permission to stay in Croatia. And there was still no solution to the conflict there.

I found myself in the middle of all these terrible events. I had lost everything I thought was mine: friends, national identity, country. I felt as if I were in a big vacuum. And there seemed to be no way for us as a family to stay together. Then my father decided to go to Vienna. We eventually joined him. For us it was a neutral place. And living in a neutral place was the only way for my family to live a normal life. But we could not earn enough money for a normal life.

I had always wanted to go to university. In high school I was an excellent student and planned to continue my education. But, all of a sudden, studying anywhere in Yugoslavia became impossible for me. When I came to Vienna, I applied to Vienna University, was accepted, and enrolled to study biochemistry, which had always been my dream.

I would like to return to my country, which I miss very much. I hope it will recover from these terrible wounds, and rise from the ashes. I would like to be there when that happens, to help my people achieve peace, democracy and justice.

I. S.
Vienna, Austria

What Is 'Home'?

My country does not exist any more. So where is *home* then? What direction does one take to *return* to Yugoslavia? I do have the desire to go to Yugoslavia, where my family still live. But what is my country now? 'Yugoslavia'?! Burned cities and friendships, destroyed lives and families...Childhood friends who have become 'national enemies', 'national heroes', warriors and murderers. Sarajevo, where I once fell in love, is now ruined by hatred. On the Adriatic coast, the most beautiful coast in the world, which I felt was part of my homeland, I am now considered an enemy. These wounds will take a long time to heal.

This is my third year in the USA, and it is still not clear to me what it would mean to face 'Yugoslavia', even though I have turned that country into the object of my studies. Why did it happen? The answer remains as distant as ever. I have been reading about comparable human experiences, fascism and the Holocaust in Germany, for example, but the question only grows and the answer becomes more and more elusive.

How do I perceive my future and the possibility of returning to my home country after completing my studies?

I am sorry to say that I cannot really answer this question. My private life and my professional interests are closely tied to 'Yugoslavia'. But as the situation now stands in Serbia and Croatia, people who oppose the war, people without prejudice towards other 'Yugoslav' nations and ethnic groups, are less than welcome. Perhaps, to *return* to Yugoslavia means to go back into the future and start recreating the peace that once existed among its nations. It is my hope that 'Yugoslavia' will one day again open its doors to everybody. I remain dedicated to realizing the hope of a 'Yugoslav' space that goes beyond national boundaries. *Home* is where the doors are open. My wish is that people like me, who left Yugoslavia because of the war, can find their place in it again.

We have no other choice than to go and reacquaint ourselves with once familiar places. No choice than to return (to places where we have never been) and let friends (whom we have never seen) into our homes (which are not yet ours). *Home* is where somebody I do not know entered first.

P. R.
Binghampton, New York, USA

I Have Always Felt Yugoslav

My main reason for leaving the country was the steadily worsening situation in the former Yugoslavia. My family has always lived in Belgrade. But my parents are ethnically 'mixed', and a lot of my relatives and friends lived in different parts of the country. Therefore I always felt Yugoslav. Nationalism, now so widespread, is extremely oppressive for me and my family. In that respect we have been badly affected by the horrible, senseless, neverending war. My two uncles, one from Belgrade and the other from Zagreb, had to flee the country forever in order to avoid being called up into the army, which would have forced them to fight on opposing sides against each other. Other relatives have also desperately tried to leave the country, because as Serbs in Croatia, or Croats in Serbia, they have lost their jobs.

Before the war I spent a lot of my time in Croatia and Slovenia, where I had many friends. Sadly, I have lost almost all contact with them, as with my relatives in other parts of the former Yugoslavia. I was unable to get in touch with them from Belgrade. It was not until I came to the US that I was able to phone some of them.

Ironical as it sounds, here in Philadelphia I have made new friendships with people from 'other parts' of the former Yugoslavia, for example with a boy from Split, Croatia, who is studying at the same university. That would be impossible in our former country at the moment.

Even though there has been no fighting in Belgrade, my home town has greatly changed. There is a heavy feeling of repression against anyone who disagrees with the present government's policy of war. The feeling of insecurity and chaos has increased. No one feels safe there any more. I remember one afternoon last year, when I was returning from school, shooting began in a street near my house, and although people ran for cover, several were injured. Such incidents occurred rather often. In the dire economic situation there things can only deteriorate.

The high school I attended in Belgrade was very good, providing me with a sound start for my further education. Unfortunately, the University of Belgrade, which I had planned to attend, was also affected by the current situation. Many, not to say almost all, of the best professors and teaching assistants left the country, and the quality of education that Belgrade University now offers is inferior to what it was before. Not to mention the fact that there is no modern equipment for laboratories, which means no possibilities for the practical application of the material one studies. So, I made my choice. I was determined to obtain a proper education, and decided that it would be best to try to enrol at a good university abroad. Since studying abroad involves great expense, I had to apply to various private institutions in the US, knowing that only they could offer me any financial aid. (Citizens of the Federal Republic of Yugoslavia are not eligible for any financial aid from government institutions here.) But it is still a burden to my family.

The high school I attended in Belgrade was designed for 'especially gifted students in the field of mathematics and the natural sciences', and it helped me to study mathematics and computer science at the University of Pennsylvania. I have deliberately chosen two majors. I have always been very interested in maths, while computer science seems such an innovative and challenging area of study.

I would be very happy to work in any part of the former Yugoslavia. I feel that it is my native country, the place where I belong. Of course, I hope that it will one day be open again to the world and to neighbouring countries, because that is the only way a state can make any progress.

L. P.
Philadelphia, Pennsylvania, USA

Yugoslavia Is Always on My Mind

The civil war in Yugoslavia changed my life dramatically. Within a matter of months the massacres and devastation began, I lost my country, and even the hope of peace and a better future. I was horrified to see how people in my native town of Bihać rose in rage against each other when political tensions overwhelmed them. I saw their faces distorted by hatred, their eyes searching for motives to raid and plunder their neighbours' homes.

Nothing to eat, nothing to hope for. If I stayed, I could do nothing but go insane with fear, hunger, despair. I had one chance—to leave my home and my parents, who felt too old to become emigrés. I did not think that I could help a country I no longer felt was mine. So I fled and came to Austria to try a better life. And to continue my studies, which I had abandoned because of the war.

My studies (English and Spanish at the University of Salzburg) have become the most important thing in my life. In these difficult times they keep me strong, and give meaning to my life. In spite of the miseries of life as a refugee, I am happy to be at university in Austria, among young people who share my interests and aspirations. Studying English and Spanish in German made me think about Europe, and European nations, about the diversity of their cultures. But Yugoslavia is always on my mind. I can't help thinking about the hatred and division between people who had lived together in peace for decades. I can't find a reason for it. I hope my studies of European culture will help me to understand not only other countries, but my own as well. I shall learn how to get along despite the antagonisms among us Serbs, Croats and Muslims.

I think about my future. I see it in terms of the future of Bosnia. That is where my home is, and I feel strongly attached to it. There is nothing better than the warm feeling of being at home in a country one belongs to. I am sure there will be an end to this war, and I wait for the day when I will be able to go back to my country, to my friends and relatives, to my people.

N. P.

Salzburg, Austria

We Shall Have to Build
a Whole New National Identity

The country's deteriorating economic and social situation not only increased the sense of insecurity among young people, but also resulted in the material and intellectual impoverishment of the educational system.

In the decades preceding the final stage of the 'Yugoslav crisis', our education was based on a mixture of carefully built hopes for the future of the Yugoslav political system and ideologically constructed 'truths' about the historical need for a common state of the southern Slavs. We knew that this state was no recent creation, that it dated from 1918. But, at the same time, we were convinced that our state's real history did not begin until the Second World War, that everything before then was just a necessary prelude to the real thing. I use the word 'necessary' deliberately, to evoke the official Yugoslav line of the late sixties and seventies, which linked the Marxist ideology of the inevitable transition of capitalism to socialism to the Titoist proclamation of 'socialism with a human face'. This version of socialism centred on the worker and on dismantling the power of the State. Unfortunately, it soon became clear that behind this supposedly humanist, egalitarian and progressive society was the huge bureaucratic apparatus of the Communist Party. Once its leader was gone the Party could no longer keep pace with its own rhetoric. It became obvious to everyone that economic hardships and inter-ethnic relations could not be explained away by recourse to the usual lingo of Party dignitaries.

It was in the eighties, after Tito's death, that I became interested in journalism and started working first for Studio B, the independent radio-station, and then for the youth press, newspapers written by and for high-school and university students. The first three to four years of my career in journalism were marked by enthusiasm for the new potential opening up for the democratization of our society. New topics were discussed, among them Tito's role in Yugoslav history, the possibilities of a multi-party system, privatization of the economy, feminist and other social issues. After those first few years, a new kind of discourse developed, first in the alternative media and then in the official media as well. A new kind of professional politician emerged and, simultaneously, the profile of journalism changed. The new political rhetoric was seemingly more democratic but, in many cases, actually more insidious in criticizing the past without knowing how to deal with the present. At the same time, the media became sharply divided between those who were for and those who were against the new rhetoric. I did not want to be a part of this atmosphere of polarization and criticism which became more and more personal, militaristic and unable to reflect on its own methods and goals. I stopped working for the radio in 1986, and continued writing for newspapers a bit longer, this time trying to write about what I thought would be the focus of my professional future: the literature and culture of the Spanish-speaking world.

Even though I enjoyed studying Spanish language and literature, I was becoming progressively more tense and pessimistic about the evolution of the new political climate, in which any kind of serious intellectual work was being marginalized. Towards the end of my studies, I became increasingly concerned about the personal and professional effects of Yugoslav, and especially Serbian, society's decline into anti-intellectualism, nationalism and a strange kind of chaos. As a child of an inter-ethnic marriage (my father is Serbian and my mother Croatian), and as a politically aware individual, I found it difficult to take sides in the multiple conflicts that were shaking Yugoslav society at the end of the eighties. It was obvious to me that these conflicts were engendering at least two dangerous political views: a blindly aggressive attitude towards anyone who was labelled an 'opponent' of the new national leadership, and an equally blind defence of the virtues of one ethnic group over others. Apart from the political climate, my family's increasingly poor economic situation seemed unlikely to improve in the next ten years. All these factors forced me to make a decision about my future. The only solution I could think of was trying to live somewhere else, completely on my own.

I think that the Yugoslav civil war has created an unhealable wound in the consciousness of all the citizens of the former Yugoslavia who have managed to survive it. This is definitely true in my case, since not only did my family become divided in the conflict, but I was forced to learn about the war via CNN in America. The only short-term solution for my feelings of guilt, anger and helplessness is to keep visiting Belgrade and to try to find some immediate connection with the events of the past four years since I left. In the long term, I think that it is absolutely vital to help rebuild that other side of the former Yugoslavia which very few people take into consideration. I mean the psychological, emotional and intellectual energy and abilities of the present and future citizens of the new states. In Serbia's case in particular, I think that international policy towards the Milošević government has completely ignored the progressive democratic initiatives which are taking place in Belgrade, or which might take place if there were some kind of interchange between non-governmental forces in Serbia and international public opinion. As someone who is a declared Yugoslav, I am ashamed of the crimes being committed in the name of some sort of mythical fatherland which the Milošević government still insists on calling Yugoslavia. What I think all citizens of this latest, crippled Yugoslavia will have to figure out is not only *who* committed the crimes, but also in the name of what kind of dangerous Yugoslav or Serbian nationhood. In other words, we will have to build a whole new national identity. I think it is a wonderful idea to try to initiate dialogue among those former Yugoslavs who had to either escape or distance themselves from their war-torn country. I see this dialogue abroad as a basis for our return to and reintegration in the life of our future countries. I think that the quality of education I have received at the University of Wisconsin and now at Duke will allow me to use my knowledge and critical skills in different ways. Duke University is an academic institution which is profoundly interested in the issues of globalization, multiculturalism and area studies. This orientation was one of the reasons for my decision to continue my studies here. So far I have had a chance to meet several intellectuals and activists from Bosnia, Slovenia, Croatia, and Yugoslavia. It has certainly broadened my outlook to be able to converse with people whose positions range from a Bosnian ethnomusicologist to the President of Slovenia. In my daily work on Spanish literature, I look at the ways in which this literature addresses the problems of a multinational state and cultural conflicts which culminated in the Spanish Civil War.

Although it is hard to know what kind of job I will be able to get in Belgrade, my goal will always be to help future generations of Yugoslavs address the problems that this war has raised. I hope to be able to work as a language teacher, as a journalist interested in the international aspects of the Yugoslav crisis, or as a translator and scholar building bridges between the Yugoslav and Hispanic cultural traditions.

T. G.

Durham, North Carolina, USA

What Do I Mean By 'My Country'?

To me my country has always meant everything people call the former Yugoslavia and, despite all the bloodshed, hatred and wasted lives, I still see no reason to change that. To contemplate the future when you carry a Yugoslav passport requires great optimism, and a belief in miracles. People unfamiliar with the Balkan mentality will never understand that.

My people and my country have spat on their young by taking from them their dreams and hopes. I want to go back, not because my country needs me, but because I need my country.

J.J.
Clausahl-Zellerfeld, Germany

I Was a Yugoslav, But Now I Am a Bosnian

It is hard to describe the atmosphere in Serbia in 1991 and 1992. There was something evil in the air, something aggressive among the people. I witnessed the beginning of radicalism and of true, genuine hatred. Most of us, especially non-Serbs, did not know what to make of the war in Croatia. But after the shelling of Dubrovnik, a city which can be compared only to Venice, things began to be clearer: this was not the defence of Yugoslavia. It became obvious who the real enemy of the people was. Then came the battle for Vukovar. For three months we watched TV pictures of the city being demolished house by house. Living in Belgrade became more and more dangerous. Every day there were shootings; soldiers coming from the front were blowing up cafés with hand-grenades; non-Serbs were mistreated. I noticed a change of behaviour in many of my friends. At first, they were small, barely noticeable things, but eventually real hostility was shown against me. One old friend of mine, who is now a member of the Radical Party, told me that he would personally beat me up if I stayed in Belgrade, or ever returned. Since then I have been working in Vienna.

My mother comes from Sarajevo, Bosnia. Her mother and relatives still live there. My father comes from Goražde, in eastern Bosnia.

The last time I was in Sarajevo was at the beginning of March 1992, three weeks before the war. I was working for Spanish Television at the time and had the chance to get a close-up view of what was really happening. I witnessed the Serb barricades and the people preparing to defend their neighbourhoods. And I remember feeling that war was about to begin. But then things seemed to calm down, and shortly afterwards I returned to Belgrade.

There, for the first time, I had trouble at the university because of my origins. A maths professor asked me what I, a Muslim, was still doing in Serbia.

The war in Bosnia began. I had just published my first book, a collection of poetry. A harmless one. Mainly my impressions from the ages of eighteen to twenty-one. Thanks to the publisher, the book got a lot of publicity. But it caused trouble: I received threatening phone calls, I was called a 'fundamentalist', and so on. My parents began to fear for me, and so I left Belgrade for good, and went back to Vienna.

I have never lived in Bosnia. I lived the first eleven years of my life in Vienna, and then the next eleven years in Belgrade. I have spent the last two years back in Vienna. I was a Yugoslav, but now I am a Bosnian with all my heart. Bosnia is a destroyed but still beautiful country. Even after all the horror, I have not become a nationalist, full of hate. I still have a lot of Serbian friends here in Vienna. But I will not return to Belgrade. It is not the city I once knew and loved. I doubt that Sarajevo will be the same either. But for Sarajevans there is still hope. And so I hope with them.

I think that people like me will one day contribute to reviving dialogue between the countries of the former Yugoslavia, bringing to them a sense of tolerance and mutual understanding. I am determined to tie my future in with the future of Bosnia, not only because of my prospects there as an engineer, but also because of my ambitions as a writer. These are historic times, and, in a way, it is exciting to be a part of them.

B. T.
Vienna, Austria

I Am a Citizen of a State That Does Not Exist

I am a member of the Romanian national minority in Vojvodina and a citizen of a Yugoslavia which no longer exists. I did not take part in its break-up, but the region I ended up living in is led by people who, in my opinion, bear the brunt of the responsibility for the civil war and its people's moral and material poverty.

When the crisis started, I was working as a bookseller in my family's private company and was a part-time student at the Faculty of Natural Sciences and Mathematics in Belgrade. With the collapse of Yugoslavia came the collapse of the economic system as well, and, no matter how hard I worked, I kept getting poorer and poorer, with diminishing chances of completing my education and earning a living. A growing number of people around me were being mobilized, the regime's propaganda was blocking out the truth, plunging the people into poverty, and life became increasingly impoverished and hard. I started feeling inundated by a wave of chauvinism. All this drove me to take advantage of my Romanian origins and to try to build myself a new life in the country of my forefathers. In the autumn of 1992 I enrolled in the Department of Electrical Engineering in Romania, but I was unable to start my studies right away for lack of funds. Also I hoped that the December elections might bring some change.

Unfortunately, the elections were rigged and those who had brought war and poverty became even more powerful and ruthless than before. Not only was there spreading poverty, but I also received my call-up papers, and was experiencing growing unpleasantness because I was not a member of the ruling party or the majority nation. My conscience would not let me put on the uniform of the wrong side, and my reason told me it was better to finish a good university than to work at a loss. And so I wound up my business and came to Romania at the beginning of 1993. I haven't been home since. My army call-up papers keep coming.

Romania is nearby, I know the language, and the subject I have chosen to study (computer sciences) offers me hope of a better future.

The future is very uncertain at the moment. After the fall of the dictatorial regime, I think a kind of Balkan economic community will be set up and Yugoslavia (i.e. the states that have emerged from it) will become a huge building site, a place for capital ventures. I see my own role as a bridge between Romania and Yugoslavia. Young, educated people with an excellent knowledge of both languages and both communities will help the region's rapid recovery and progress. That is where I see my chance to be useful.

N. L.
Timisoara, Romania

One Day We Shall All Live in Harmony

After completing high school I applied to the School of Medicine at the University of Prishtina. But I was turned down. The school was very competitive, with a large number of applicants for a small number of places. And so I went abroad.

I was admitted to a Medical School. I hoped that after a year or two I would be able to continue my studies back home. However, after I left, the situation in the former Yugoslavia became much worse, making it impossible for me to go back. The difficult economic, social and political situation, coupled with the ethnic conflicts engulfing Yugoslavia, forced me to remain outside the country, even though my financial resources were insufficient to sustain me. My parents are unemployed, and I am entirely dependent on help from my relatives.

I was forced to stay away from my family and friends. But I hope that I shall soon be able to return and lead a normal life again. I am positive that one day we shall all live like other human beings in this world.

The worsening situation in the former Yugoslavia is the main reason which keeps me here in a foreign land. There are three reasons why it would have been much easier for me to study in my homeland:

First, the School of Medicine is located in my home town, so my living expenses would not be so high;

Second, the language of instruction would have been Albanian, my mother tongue, and I would not have to struggle with a language that is completely foreign to me;

Third, if I had been able to study in my native country, I would have observed and learned more about diseases which are common to my people and the area I come from.

Nevertheless, despite being in a foreign country I still hope that I will go back one day. *Dum spiro spero*: As long as I breathe, I hope. Like all other citizens of the former Yugoslavia, I think that the future will be better and happier for all of us. Ethnic conflict cannot go on forever. One day we shall extend one another the hand of friendship and live together in harmony and peace, like truly free human beings. I see my future as strongly linked to the future of my native land. I owe a great deal to the land of my birth, the land where I grew up. And I have a moral responsibility to go back and do something for its people.

Where I come from, Kosova, poverty is woven all through our lives. Diseases kill people by the thousands, diseases which belong to the past, and which are not common in modern-day Europe. The infant mortality rate is very high, contagious diseases proliferate at a time when children in Europe have all the conditions to live healthy, happy lives. All these and other reasons (stemming from the horrors taking place in our corner of the world) morally bind me to go home after I have completed my studies. I shall do my best to help my country and my people. To quote an Albanian saying: 'Drop by drop fills the well.' Which means: If everybody does his (or her) bit, we can make our country a better place to live in, and improve the situation in the whole of the former Yugoslavia.

N. K.
Switzerland

Pictures in My Mind

My name is L. N. and I was born in Sarajevo on 12 July 1971. I had a carefree, happy childhood, and I associate Sarajevo with the best time of my life.

I would like just quickly to paint you a picture of what Sarajevo was like before this cursed war (a picture which is always in my mind).

I grew up surrounded by children of all nationalities (Serbs, Croats and Muslims). I never really knew the meaning of nationality. We all felt the same, we were Yugoslavs. It never mattered what nationality you were. It is this cursed war that has divided and killed people.

Having travelled all over Yugoslavia with my father (a professor at the Music Academy in Sarajevo) I was able to admire its many wonders. Yugoslavia is indescribably beautiful. I use the name Yugoslavia quite deliberately, because I find it hard to accept that it is now so divided.

My mother is a translator of English and my older sister studies Serbo-Croatian language and literature. I did my military service with the Yugoslav People's Army (JNA) from September 1990 to September 1991, where I made lots of friends. The fact that we were together twenty-four hours a day made us all like brothers. The war broke out in June 1991 and I started worrying that I might find myself in a situation where I would have to shoot at one of my brothers (perhaps by chance, perhaps not). The thought upset me so much that I decided to leave the country for a while, to study abroad and come back later.

Because of my Jewish roots I had the opportunity to emigrate to Israel. The state of Israel helps new immigrants with their studies, which is my main reason for being here. I desperately want to finish my studies and then to return to my Yugoslavia. I miss my parents and sister terribly. I haven't seen them for two and a half years. There were times when I didn't hear from them for months. I worry about them. I miss Sarajevo and all my good friends who are still there. I miss the landscape. I miss everything.

I'm majoring in political science so that when I return home I'll be able to help rebuild and develop political life there and contribute to the process of guiding it towards peace, democracy, freedom and fundamental human rights. I shall work to reconcile all the nations so that one day we can all live together in peace and brotherhood, like the picture in my mind.

L. N.
Tel Aviv, Israel

Chapter 8: **Hopes and Wishes**

I Feel I Have Started All Over Again

In March 1992, when I returned, homesick and delighted, from London (where I had been for half a year), I never even dreamed that I would soon be leaving again. And for a much, much longer time, leaving not only my home and country, but the whole of my life. (My home town of Zvornik, where I was staying, was attacked on 8 April 1992 and occupied soon afterwards. I had to flee. None of us had a choice. My parents followed me. We are now in Vienna, Austria. Many people from my home town are now in Austria, others are scattered all over the world.)

Two years later, after long months of feeling lost and depressed (like so many other refugees), I plucked up the courage and strength to start again. I did it by going back to university. Having made the decision, I feel I have started all over again. I now study Spanish, a beautiful language. (My first real contact with it was as a student in Sarajevo.) As for Spanish literature, I can only say that for me it is an enormous pleasure to read, and an irresistible challenge to study.

However, I must admit that since my life fell apart so suddenly and violently two years ago—as did so many lives!—I have not had any clear, properly thought-out plans for my future; instead I have learned to take things as they come. But I do know that my greatest wish is to return to my country and my home, and to give the best of myself to help restore life and happiness to that once beautiful country.

A. T.

Vienna, Austria

I Hope...

I graduated from Sarajevo University in 1988, and started to work for one of the biggest commercial companies in Bosnia. My husband was employed by the same company and in 1989 was sent to Great Britain to do his PhD. In the summer of 1991, I took a one-year leave of absence and joined him. A few months later, the war started in Yugoslavia. Slowly but surely it closed in on our town. Here in Britain we watched, in disbelief, as the evil forces of nationalism destroyed our country. We could not believe that something like that could ever happen to our country, to our city, where we had lived so happily.

All of a sudden, we had to face the grim reality that a war was raging in our country, our parents' lives were in danger, our home was destroyed. Now all we can do is wait...

While waiting, I would like to improve my skills and my knowledge. So I have enrolled in a MSc course in air transport management. These studies did not exist in the former Yugoslavia, and there is a shortage of experts in the field. Air transport has played a decisive role in aid delivery and has helped to save many human lives in this war. It will be equally crucial in the peacetime process of rebuilding the country. Links with the rest of the world will be essential for the development of a modern, civilized society. Because of the scale of the destruction, it will be difficult in the beginning to organize effective road and rail transport, and here air transport will have a significant role to play.

I hope that, when all the horrors of this war become nothing but a painful memory, the people of my country will be able to offer tourists a pleasant holiday destination, as they did before the war.

I hope that the people of my country will soon come to realize that we all have to live together and to cooperate, as we did for centuries past. Of course, there are some cultural and religious differences between us, but we should be wise enough to see them as an advantage, not use them as a means of division.

I hope—as do most of my good friends who managed to escape the horrors of war—that one day we shall all be able to go back and help rebuild our towns and our lives.

S. V.
London, UK

I Have Only My Knowledge to Offer

In the course of 1991 Yugoslavia became a country without a president or government, without clear borders or a political system; in short a country without the basic attributes of a modern European state. There was no end to this misfortune in sight. Fear and a sense of disorientation prevailed. Plans for the future lost all meaning, and the will to work lost its purpose. Everything became temporary. Given the situation, it seemed pointless to continue my studies. In the summer of 1991 I decided to leave Yugoslavia and go to France.

My reasons for leaving the country were moral as well as professional.

First of all, I had never had anything to do with politics, nor did I believe that problems, especially state problems, could be resolved by force. Almost overnight the country I had known became the past, and instead of arguing with words, people began reaching for weapons. Unable to change anything, the only thing left for a civilized person to do in such a situation was to withdraw.

I grew up in a family which never judged anyone by their nationality or political conviction, and I couldn't identify with this new value system which divided people into 'good' and 'bad', 'ours' and 'theirs', fascist 'democrats' and undemocratic 'fascists'.

Raised in a Christian family, I felt unable to point a gun at anyone who spoke the same language and carried the same passport as me. The army had taught me to defend my country against foreigners, but not against my erstwhile brothers.

Lastly, since I am not good with guns, and do not know much about democracy, the only way I think I can serve my country is professionally. I have devoted a third of my life to my profession, and if my mind and life serve me well, I shall devote the rest of my life to it as well. I have nothing else to offer my country.

A. M.
Paris, France

I Have Often Wondered
What My Friends Feel and Think

When I think of the war in my homeland, I often wish I could turn the clock back. I know that is impossible, but I also know I have many beautiful memories of the first eighteen years of my life, which I spent in Sarajevo. It is those memories that allow me to picture myself in the Sarajevo of 1990. I had just returned from a three-week trip to England. That was the first time I had been away from my family. It was a wonderful experience. It gave me a taste of what it is like to live in a foreign country. One day we were at my grandparents'. My whole family was there, curious to hear all about my trip. Somewhere in the middle of our conversation my mother said: 'Maybe next year we'll send you to America for a year.' I remember laughing at the idea, thinking my mother was joking. Needless to say, for the next month or so not a day went by when I did not think of my mother's words. The idea fascinated me as much as it scared me. At first I thought that there was no way I could leave my family and friends for a whole year. But the more I thought about it and the more I talked about it with my friends and family, the more excited I became about the whole idea. I realized that it was something I wanted to do and that was definitely worth experiencing. I knew that going to the United States for a year would be an experience I would treasure for the rest of my life. So, in August 1991 I packed my things, said goodbye to my family and friends, and embarked on a journey to new places and new faces. And how exciting it has been! I feel that the year I spent as an exchange student in northern Kentucky has changed me in different ways. It has defined the person I have become. It has opened up my mind to a lot of things. It has helped me look at the war in my country from a different perspective. I realize how important tolerance, openmindedness and universal acceptance are. Those used to be just words to me, but now they are the rules I live by.

When the war in Bosnia began, my time in the United States was slowly coming to an end. At least that is how it was supposed to be. I remember those couple of months in the spring of 1992 as being very upsetting and frustrating. There I was, an ocean away from the people I loved most, not knowing what the future would bring. One thing was certain; I could not go back to Sarajevo. Thinking about it makes me sad even now. I had so much looked forward to going back.

I wanted to share my wonderful and exciting experiences with my family and friends. I wanted those closest to me to meet me at the airport with open arms. Instead, I had to worry about my own future.

I had always planned on going to college, and I knew that I could make that wish come true if I were to stay in the United States. I was very lucky to have the support of many people. My parents, though far away and virtually cut off from the rest of the world, were my biggest source of encouragement. Just thinking of them and knowing that what I was doing with my life would make them very proud gave me strength and hope.

I am almost halfway through my undergraduate college career, and it still seems as if only yesterday I was just a teenager whose favourite things in life were family skiing trips to the mountains outside Sarajevo, splendid summer holidays on the Adriatic coast, playing the piano in the quiet of our home in Sarajevo, or just going dancing with my friends. I think of those times often, and in my heart I know I always will. The war in my country may have taken a lot of things away from me, but it can never take my memories. It can never take away the person I have become, one who will always remember what it was like to live in a beautiful country called Yugoslavia, to have friends of many different nationalities, and be proud of calling herself a Yugoslav.

Now that I have two more years of study at Transylvania University, which has become my home away from home, I often think about what the future will bring. Sometimes it scares me because I feel as though I am living from one year to the next. The hardest question anyone could ask me would be: Where do I see myself five years hence? I wish my answer could be something simple like: 'Oh, I am going home to be happily reunited with my family and friends.' But, I know it is not as simple as that. I have lost contact with so many of my friends. I still dream about getting together with all of them. Maybe some day that will happen, but there is so much work to be done first.

Since I cannot predict my future, or the future of my country, I will tell you about my hopes and wishes. As I am now studying biology and psychology, I would like to continue my education on a more specialized level. The one thing I know is that whatever career I pursue in life, it will revolve around people. My main goal in life is to help others. At the moment, I am thinking about going into genetic counselling, an area of human genetics that is relatively new in the field of science and medicine. I would primarily like to help children because they are the future of the world. It hurts me deeply when I think of all the children in my country, and how many of them have died. Those who survive the war do not have very much to look forward to. Their childhood is being taken away from them and they do not even realize it. Babies are being born with diseases due to their mothers' wartime malnutrition. Babies conceived during rape, a very common case in the war-torn territories of the former Yugoslavia, are being abandoned by their young mothers. Couples who might want to adopt them will want to know whether they were born with any hereditary diseases. A genetic counsellor would help families with these sorts of problems by explaining what faces them and what choices they have. This is something I would like to do. I have also thought about becoming a doctor, and that is still something I might do later on. Taking care of the survivors of the war sounds very rewarding. The mere thought that I could be helping someone from my country warms my heart.

I have often wondered what my friends who are going through the horrors of war feel and think. Are they fighting for their lives, or are they losing hope? What would I do if I were in their shoes? Whenever I think about them, I feel almost guilty for not being there. But then I know I cannot allow myself to think that way. I prefer to think that there is a reason why I am here, in the United States of America, right now. I am here because those dearest to me cannot be here. I am here to learn and educate myself so that one day, when I am reunited with them, whenever that may be, we can share my knowledge and their experience. Until that day comes, I shall be working with all my energy, dreaming and wishing for a better tomorrow.

N. P.
Lexington, Kentucky, USA

I Want to Talk About My Studies, Not About Whether My Father Is a Croat or Not

Nothing was supposed to hinder my education, but it started under an unlucky star...

It was a time of great social upheaval; long-forgotten emblems were dragged out of damp cellars, new flags were sewn, suddenly one had to be nationally identified...

Everything we had learned in school about brotherhood and unity, about the national liberation struggle, became a lie...Friends and acquaintances started boasting about grandfathers who had been Ustashas...skeletons hidden deep inside family closets became the new national heroes.

The joy of passing my entrance exam and enrolling in college gave way to confusion and anxiety. The political situation overshadowed everything else.

When the first MIGs and tanks approached Ljubljana on 26 June 1991, my confusion turned to fear. Our exams were postponed, no one knew for how long. Various questions arose of themselves:

Where would I be able to resume my studies?

Would I have to pay for them, since overnight I had become a foreigner?

Would young professors stay on at the faculty?

Would I have to go to Zagreb to continue my studies, and how? The front line was just a few kilometres from Zagreb. My colleagues in Zagreb were taking their exams in shelters...

In the spring of 1992, I got a chance to continue my studies in Germany.

College is now the centre of my little universe. Germany offers its students immense possibilities: there are various institutions geared exclusively to students, from the student secretariat to kindergartens. But the most important thing, the thing that made it possible for me to study in Germany, is being allowed to think with my own head, to decide what is essential for my education and what is not.

Here I feel free, unhindered. Studies in Germany are not only of a higher quality, but also more international. I have friends from all over the world—from Canada to Algeria to Japan. I talk with them about our studies, not about whether my father is a Croat or not...

It is not easy to write, talk or think about the future, especially the future of the Balkans, where people no longer know the meaning of the word, because they are fighting for bare survival in the here and now. It takes a certain amount of optimism and good faith, not to say idealism, to contemplate the future in the present situation.

I think about my immediate future, which is less blurred, and easier to put into a time-frame. I have another two years until I graduate. After that I'd like to finish my studies in political science.

I see the diplomatic service as offering me a career. I want to work to improve the political situation of the ordinary man.

I'm often asked whether I'll return home after I graduate.

Will I have realistic employment opportunities?

Will there be jobs for western-educated people?

Will a job at home enable me to do more than just cover my minimum existential needs? Will there be money in the house for things like the theatre?

Will it be a country where I'll be able to move freely?

Will it be a country with freedom of expression?

Will it be a country free from the fear of potential enemies and the fear of itself?

And thousands of similar questions…

It's impossible to answer them right now. The period of upheaval is not yet over. The political situation keeps changing from one day to the next, like the inflation curve. On Monday the inflation rate was 70 per cent, on Wednesday 150 per cent, and on Friday the state issued a new convertible currency. The next Monday the game begins anew. Yet, in spite of everything, one continues to hope; like Don Quixote one pushes forward in the prosaic world of windmills…

Will I return home?

Yes, I think about returning. I hope that by the time I graduate the answers to my questions will be positive.

If they are not, then I'll have to roll up my sleeves and, using everything I have learned here and have yet to learn, try to find positive answers—if not for us, then for those who come after us…

A. L.

Mannheim, Germany

'Sarajevo Will Remain, the Rest Will Pass'

I was born in Sarajevo, and lived most of my life there. As I grew up, I fell in love with the city and its people. It is a city where East meets West. The Roman, Byzantine, Ottoman and Austro-Hungarian empires all left their mark on the city, on its culture, on the way people live. The city itself is like a living being, with a soul. And it is that soul I loved the most.

The first time I was away from Sarajevo for more than a couple of weeks was when I went to America as an exchange student. I wanted to improve my English and experience a different culture. Travel had always been important in my family, and going to the US was the ultimate in travel to me. My dreams came true in May 1991, when I found out that I had been accepted by the AISE (American Inter-Cultural Student Exchange). I landed at Chicago airport on 19 August 1991. I was placed in Apple Valley, Minnesota, to live with the Toby family.

The school I attended was very different from my school in Sarajevo. But that posed no problem. On the contrary, I enjoyed it very much, and finished it as an honour graduate. However, by the end of the school year the war in Bosnia had broken out, and all my hopes of returning home were shattered. My parents, brother and sister were in Sarajevo. Six months later they were thrown out of their home by the Serbian military. I watched the destruction on TV. I kept asking myself: Why? What had those people done to deserve that?

Since there was no way of going home, I started looking for schools in Minnesota. But I was late. The scholarships were gone, and the good schools were full. I had no money, nor did my family. My parents had become refugees, and I had to help them. Still, I managed to enrol at Inver Hills Community College. It was a struggle to get through those times, and I do not want to quit now.

It is very important for me to complete my education. And after the war it will be very important for Bosnia to have the educated people of my generation. Most of us have suffered educationally as well. Schools and colleges have been closed down. Many students have been killed, many of the teachers who taught them are also dead, many schools have been destroyed. I am one of the privileged. And the least

I can do is take advantage of it, and finish my school, so that later on I shall be able to help those who have not been so lucky.

As for going back to Bosnia, there are several factors that will play a decisive role. If the people of Sarajevo remain united as they have been up to now, if Bosnia remains Bosnia and not just a remnant of what it once was, and if it continues to be home to all those who have lived on its soil despite the power-hungry criminals who wanted to divide them—then I shall be going back. Sarajevo is my home. It is a city one can only wish to live in. Those who could not stand to see people living together, who were envious, were bound to destroy it. But as a wartime rock song says: 'Sarajevo will remain, the rest will pass'. One day, the war will be over, and Sarajevo will still be there, waiting for me.

B. K.

Apple Valley, Minnesota, USA

I Pray to God for an Opportunity to Continue My Music Education

I come from Sarajevo, where I was born and educated. I studied music at the Sarajevo Music Academy. Sarajevo was my home until October 1992. My family lived a comfortable life in Mostar. My father worked as a civil engineer, and my mother was a teacher of chemistry. No members of my family were involved in political life.

Shortly after the war started, I left Sarajevo to join my family in Mostar. Little did we know at the time that Mostar would be subjected to vicious bombing and that we should have to flee and become refugees.

With help from my friends, my brother and I arrived in Britain. My parents were forced to leave Mostar as well, and they went to Norway.

I left my home and my country because my life was in danger, and there was nothing left for me to do in Sarajevo. I could not accept a senseless, violently imposed division of my country along national lines. I was saddened and angered by the loss of so many innocent lives, and by the wanton destruction of my city. As a musician I felt desperate, because there was little I could do to ease the burden and suffering of my fellow citizens. Now I am a refugee. But I pray to God for an opportunity to continue my music education in this country. It has always been my ambition to dedicate my career to baroque music and the harpsichord. I feel this is now a unique opportunity for me to fulfil my ambitions and complete my education.

A. P.
London, UK

I Can Only Hope That Peace Will Prevail

To explain why I left Yugoslavia, I have to go back many years before I was born.

My father is a Serb. In 1942, during the Second World War, he was sent as a small child to a concentration camp, together with many others, simply because he was a Serb. He suffered, and saw much suffering, until he was liberated by the Russian army. As an orphan he was then taken to Russia, where he lived until 1956. After returning to Bosnia, he worked as a teacher in a local school in Lopare, a small town in northern Bosnia, and married. My mother was a chemist, of Muslim background, from Tuzla. I was born in 1968.

I wanted to become a pharmacist myself, and after finishing high school I enrolled at the Faculty of Pharmacy at Belgrade University. Whilst I was studying in Belgrade, my parents divorced and my mother moved back to her home town.

When the political problems began to intensify in the late 1980s, no one could predict they would bring such horrible events in their wake. In my town of Lopare, people tried to stay together until the very last moment. When the Bosnian government scheduled the referendum on independence, it became clear that war was imminent. Serbs like my father, who had suffered in the Second World War, could not accept an independent Bosnia, led by Muslims and Croats, as had happened in the last war. Muslims, however, had their own tradition;

they felt as if they were under oppressive Serbian domination, and passionately wanted an independent state. I could understand both viewpoints, but all I wanted was a peaceful country.

In 1992 I was completing the third year of my degree in pharmacy in Belgrade when the war broke out in Bosnia. The borders were closed, and I was isolated from my family. I was scared and without any financial support to continue my studies. People thought the war would soon spread throughout Yugoslavia. I had a friend in London who invited me to join her there. I accepted the invitation, and left the country. Once in the UK, I tried to continue my education. Now I am reading pharmacy at Queen's University, Belfast.

Although my future, like that of my country, is very uncertain, I hope I shall be reunited with my family in Bosnia. I would love to practise my skills and knowledge at home. Whether that will happen in the near future depends on events beyond my control. I can only hope that peace will prevail.

J. Dj.
Belfast, UK

I Find It Difficult to Answer Your Questions

I am pleased to know that there is growing concern for students and promising young people from the former Yugoslavia, and for their country's future. I hope that a large number of students, willing to complete their studies and gain experience from the countries to which they have been displaced by the war, will be provided with adequate help, so as to achieve the aim of the whole programme—the rebirth of our country in every possible way.

But I find it difficult to answer questions about how I got out of the besieged city of Sarajevo, or what my plans were when I found myself far away from my family (I have not seen my parents or sister for nearly two years) and from the lifestyle I was accustomed to. Neither I nor any member of my family wanted to take part in this deplorable war. We did not want to join any of the parties which were formed, only to bring even worse confusion among people who had grown up together, regardless of their national, religious or other beliefs.

After much suffering, I found myself in England, where I began to work as an au pair. After many months of working hard for two families I decided that the best option for my future would be to continue the studies I had begun in Sarajevo. I passed the auditions for several music colleges at the University of London, but as I had no financial support the places were given to other students. In September 1993 I was invited by the BBC Radio World Service to take part in a discussion on the radio. I was asked to explain the difficulties our students encounter in their attempts to continue their education. I used the opportunity to ask for understanding, demanding a second chance for those who really wanted to succeed professionally, not only for their own sake, but for the sake of their country. Having heard the programme on the radio, Professor T.C. from Roehampton Institute invited me to audition for a BA music degree course. I was accepted into the second year of that course, free of charge.

Although I am very grateful to the staff of Roehampton Institute for covering my tuition fees for this three-year course, I have not yet resolved the crucial problem of living expenses, travel expenses, not to mention the books and academic material I need for my work. Moreover, as a pianist I need to buy a second-hand piano, or a digital piano.

Apart from studying to be a performing pianist and accompanist, I am also involved in a project which explores and presents the folk music tradition of the countries of the former Yugoslavia. It involves a lot of travelling, because of personal contacts with ethnomusicologists and experts who are also displaced and sometimes difficult to locate, not to mention the rare books and academic material that have to be bought.

That is why I so need your help.

I. C.
London, UK

Post Scriptum

Letter to a Sarajevo Generation

This letter is addressed to Sarajevo refugees, especially to one specific category of them: the generation born in 1973–74. To the generation who, unfortunately, will remember their senior year of high school as a bad dream, instead of the best year of their student life. To the first generation after the Second World War to be denied its graduation ceremony, one of the most exciting and important events of one's high-school career. This letter is addressed to you, because I myself, born in 1974, belong to the graduating class of 1992.

'I remember it as if it were yesterday,' Dr Nele Karajlić sang in one of his songs. Almost two and a half years ago now, some thirty Sarajevo high-school students, including myself, went to the United States as part of a student exchange programme. All of us with identical feelings of anxiety and uncertainty over the unknown, but also with enthusiasm for something new and exciting. Happy, because we were beginning the greatest adventure of our lives. Sad, because we were leaving our classmates, our desks and chairs, and missing the graduation ceremony and ball; because we had to say goodbye to unforgettable nights out in Sarajevo in front of the National Theatre, to famous discotheques like Theatre, CDA, AG, Red Gallery, BB, KUK, Unity…We were leaving the concerts of Zabranjeno pušenje, EKV, Azra…The last days before our departure we went to school to experience one last time the unique atmosphere of Sarajevo high schools and to say a last goodbye to our classmates and teachers. On our last night we went out to feel once more the seductive fragrance of Sarajevo's summer nights, showered with stars and filled with thousands of young people. For the last time, we said goodbye to friends and exchanged secret looks full of hidden significance with those who used to be more than just friends, those who represented the most beautiful days of our student lives. The next morning, after a sleepless night, we boarded the plane which would take us to uncertainty, thousands of miles away. We couldn't control the tears mercilessly trickling down our cheeks, as we said goodbye to our parents and closest friends. Just then, for some unknown reason, we envied everyone who was staying, everyone who would be attending the graduation ceremony, the transition from carefree school-days to the experience of real life, a symbolic transition from childhood to maturity. In our minds, we were already ten months ahead, returning to Sarajevo, seeing our beloved city again after a long, long time.

What has happened in the meantime need not be described. It began with the first three quiet months (when we all still thought there were only seven more months until our return); then came the disturbing news about the situation in the country in January and February 1992 and the first incomprehensible war scenes in other parts of the former Yugoslavia that we saw on TV and in the newspapers; and finally the trauma and tragedy which started in April and May, which we lived in our minds, with the same intensity as our families back home, if not worse. Those were the painful moments when we started to realize that our much longed-for return home was becoming more and more distant, more and more unreal. Ironically, in June 1992 we had the 'privilege' of participating in the graduation ceremony and officially completing high school, unlike our Sarajevo schoolmates. We were lucky not to hear bombs and snipers, not to see demolished buildings and destroyed streets, but to remember Sarajevo in the most beautiful way. Isolated from the painful atmosphere of insane, meaningless national hatred, in our hearts we have remained *Yugoslavs*, thinking not of Serbs, Croats and Muslims, but of our *friends* in our homeland. Isolated from personal experience of a physically and morally ruined Sarajevo, we have still remained *Sarajevans*—a concept which is impossible to describe in words, but familiar to anyone who has spent at least a period of their life in this unique and once beautiful city, a city surrounded by the Olympic mountains of Jahorina, Bjelašnica, Igman and Romanija, a city which possessed a magic atmosphere in its spring rain, summer sun, and cold, starry winter nights. A city which had a soul.

What has happened to our dreams? What has happened to our thoughts and plans for the future, our ideals, which each one of us once followed with enthusiasm, the secret wishes somewhere deep inside every one of us? All of them have been buried, erased, they have vanished without a trace, with no sign of return. Most of the questions that we ever asked about our future have now lost all sense, and seem like a dream we dreamed a long time ago. Reality has enveloped everyone in a grey, gloomy shroud, with no sign of setting them free. Everything seems tired and listless, as after a long period of hibernation, from which one won't, or can't, wake up.

And now, after more than two years, the only question I ask myself (I have given up all others—they seem too idealistic) is: What next? What will happen to Sarajevo and its former and present inhabitants? What is the future of thousands of young people, people whose youth has been destroyed by the shocks of war and the psychotic atmosphere of sick ethnic hatred? What will happen to us, after being separated from our parents for more than two years, with no hope of seeing them again soon? I talk to my mother on the phone once a week (she is now a refugee in Belgrade, Yugoslavia), but recently those conversations, our only way of communicating in the past couple of years, have become tense, brief and unfinished because of the astronomical cost of overseas calls. Unfinished, but precious, more precious than anything else. I'd give anything in the world for one brief, unfinished conversation with my father, whom I have not heard from in more than a year and a half. I do not know whether he is still in Sarajevo, whether he is still alive and whether I shall ever see him again. I should like to tell him that I love him, that I think of him every day, and that he shouldn't worry about me, because I am all right—at least better than he is. I know he would be proud of me, knowing that I have managed to make my way in this distant world and continue my college career. I should like so much to let him know about my grades and experiences, and to hear his voice again one more time. I do not know whether I ever shall.

Lately almost all my dreams have started turning into tense thrillers with uncertain endings; all of them are related to my family, friends, Sarajevo. Every morning I expect to wake up from a long and painful nightmare, and see the familiar walls of my room and beloved face of my mother, who will assure me it was all a bad dream—just like long ago, when I was a little girl. Instead, I see an empty room, surrounded by the walls of the university dormitory, which sometimes seem unfamiliar and cold. At such moments, the dream becomes reality, and the much-awaited moment of waking up fades, along with the ugly scenes of the dream. As time passes, I am becoming aware that no dream can be this hard and this long, that only reality can be so cruel. And that realization hurts. Abnormally. Inhumanly. Indescribably.

I often wonder what have we done wrong to deserve a youth

like this, full of convulsions and uncertainties. They tell us we are young, that our whole life lies ahead of us. But nobody mentions our ruined childhood, lives deprived of a carefree youth, which our parents had. Many who are still in the former Yugoslavia think that for those of us who had the chance to leave before the beginning of the war, things are easier, because we were spared the war. Yes, we didn't get to see scary pictures of a demolished country and painful scenes of people bleeding and dying in the streets and in their homes. True, in that way we were the most fortunate people in the world. But, although we were lucky to avoid scenes of war, we were forced to grow up too soon in today's big, cruel world; we were left all alone, without parents, who are the only ones we know really love us, and really care whether or not we make our way in the world. No matter how much we used to believe, as teenagers, that we could live by ourselves, without our parents—we were wrong. Every day I feel nostalgic for everything that linked me to the place where I was born and grew up, for the true, unconditional support of my parents and friends.

Somewhere deep inside me I have this hope, this strong belief, which grows every day and helps me get through the tough times. I hope so much that, after the war is over, our Sarajevo generation will have a chance to meet somewhere—as in the good old times of our evening get-togethers—and celebrate our Sarajevo high-school graduation, something we were deprived of. I hope we will have a chance to be together again, unburdened by national hatred, to look at each other not as people of different nationalities, but as *friends* with whom we shared the same classrooms; I hope that we will be able to go to the movies, go out and enjoy life's simple pleasures—just as before this war, which started beyond our sphere of influence and is being waged against our will. I live in the hope, in the dream, that everybody will stay unchanged, and that one day we will continue building our futures, picking up where we stopped.

This is, maybe, the only dream that I want to become reality. We are strong enough to make it come true.

And if we do achieve it, we shall never let anyone wake us up again. We must not. Otherwise, everything we have ever had will be lost, irretrievably.

M. S.
Gainesville, Florida, USA

DATE DUE			
GAYLORD	No. 2333		PRINTED IN U.S.A.